NEEDLEPOINT
COLLECTION

NEEDLEPOINT
COLLECTION

KAREN ELDER

IN ASSOCIATION WITH THE VICTORIA AND ALBERT MUSEUM

ANAYA PUBLISHERS LTD

LONDON

First published in Great Britain in 1992 by
Anaya Publishers Ltd, Strode House
44–50 Osnaburgh Street, London NW1 3ND

Editor Diana Brinton
Designer Edwin Belchamber
Illustrator Conny Jude
Styled photography by Linda Burgess
Additional styling by Gilly Love

British Library Cataloguing in Publication Data
Elder, Karen
V&A Needlepoint Collection
I. Title
746.44
ISBN 1-85470-124-X

Typeset by Servis Filmsetting Ltd, Manchester
Colour reproduction by Scantrans Pte Ltd, Singapore
Printed and bound in Hong Kong by Dai Nippon

CONTENTS

INTRODUCTION

*Previous page:
Prince Albert (left)
and Queen Victoria
(right) are two
cushion designs
derived from textile
patterns in the
V&A archives.

Facing page:
A detail from the
Candle Firescreen
shows how a
variety of stitches
are used to add
interest to large
blocks of single
colour. The design
(see pages 52–57) is
from an 18th-
century silk
weaving pattern by
James Leman.*

London's Victoria and Albert Museum, affectionately known as the V&A, exists to increase the understanding and enjoyment of arts, crafts and design through its collections. It was founded following the Great Exhibition of 1851, and from the start it served as a model for decorative arts and crafts museums around the world, collecting examples of contemporary excellence a well as objects of historical importance. It is a living design museum that stages fascinating exhibitions and beautifully researched showings of international collections and antiquities. Its six miles of galleries contain over five million works of art, including the National Collections of sculpture, water colours, photography and portrait miniatures. You can get lost in rooms of European ceramics, German silverware, contemporary jewellery, or the famous costume gallery. The display galleries gather together furniture, textiles, ceramics and all varieties of objects d'art – categorized by country or period – whereas the study galleries specialize in particular materials, allowing the visitor to explore and discover within narrower fields. The textile study gallery, for example, consists of hundreds of pull-out files of glass-mounted fabrics, laces and embroideries through which you can browse at your leisure.

These ever-growing collections have inspired the visually aware since the museum was founded, and every type of artist and designer looks at those objects and archives with eyes that translate them into uses for their own particular needs. Laura Ashley began printing textiles in 1953 and went on to market all over the world her own style and concept of English country life furnishings. Much of her design inspiration was derived from the museum's collections, and yet how differently American knitting and needlepoint designer, Kaffe Fassett, observed and drew upon the same source material. Prince Albert's intention when he conceived the idea of the museum was that it should lead the way, through example, toward better design in industry. In these retrospective times we sometimes forget to move forward and are happier copying things from the past than creating designs of our own times. However, re-creating beautiful patterns has its place, particularly where the period charm is strong, so I have included re-workings of old pieces that are very close to the original, along with some adaptations of textile designs to make them suitable for needlepoint, and a number of unashamedly new designs that have been inspired by objects and collections at the V&A.

The difficulty for me was where to begin. There was no shortage of ideas but to choose one century, country or discipline would have failed to represent the enormous scope that the museum offers to design enthusiasts. How could I make a cohesive book of needlepoint pieces based on such varied genres as Coptic weaving, stained glass, Victorian wallpapers, and eighteenth-century silk designs? The answer I came up with was to choose individual items that are

stunning from all centuries, regardless of geography, and to put them in a loose chronological order, taking us from fourth-century Egypt to nineteenth-century Germany, via Japan, India, and England. What these items have in common is their suitability for adaptation into designs that will enhance almost any modern home.

We start with one of my favourites, Coptic Bird, which is virtually a copy (scaled up) of a piece of ancient weaving. Those rich, bright colours are no twentieth-century invention – the Egyptians loved them back in the fourth century. The amazing thing is that the vibrancy of this

A Pheasant is one of the stitched creatures from the Oxburgh Hangings. His tail is too long for the panel, so has been brutally rearranged.

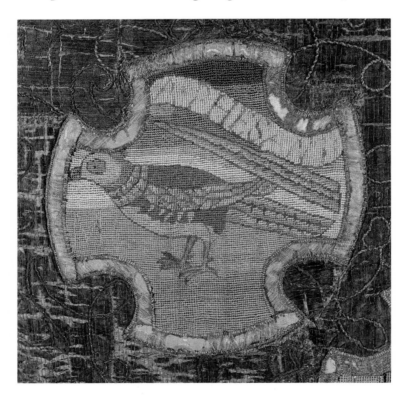

particular piece has survived the centuries. It is on display at the museum and well worth going to see and marvel at.

The next designs are taken from the famous Oxburgh hangings, stitched by Mary Queen of Scots and Bess of Hardwick, and familiar to many from the museum's postcards. One of the most exciting discoveries for me was the Bradford

Table Carpet which, as its name suggests, is a canvaswork carpet designed to cover a huge table. Its enormous illustrated border is full of animals, buildings, people, trees, and happenings. There was only room for two snippets from this carpet but I would love to have done more.

In 1990 the V&A held an exhibition of eighteenth-century silk-weaving designs. Those of Anna Maria Garthwaite and James Leman excited me particularly, and the archives produced some fantastic patterns that inspired five of the designs in this book. The long stitch chair seat cover, in contrast, is a translation into needlepoint of the blocks of almost pure colour that hit the eye in the stained glass gallery. Here, beautiful stained glass windows are set in darkened walls and back-lit, as in a church, making you see each colour both in isolation and as part of a larger scheme.

From Japanese stencils came the patterns for the two blue-and-white cushions, and a wallpaper border is the basis for a design named Double Damask. Other designs are derived from collections rather than individual items. Endpaper catalogues, patterns for printed and woven textiles, and Moghul architectural drawings provided just some of the starting points from which I have set out to create new designs.

I cannot remember a time when I did not have some piece of needlework on the go, but did not discover needlepoint until I was about thirty, when a friend started me off on a stitch sampler with a piece of blank canvas and some wool. I have hardly stopped stitching since. I soon found that I could produce designs for needlepoint, though I cannot draw well and have never tried to paint. Somehow I can get results with my needle that elude me in other media. Photocopying has helped enormously, as it enables one to

Colour is a whole new subject. Discovering how to put wool colours together is perhaps the most exciting and challenging part, for what looks pretty in the hand is not automatically successful when stitched. I learned not always to choose colours that I liked as individuals, for odd colours often point up other shades to their best advantage. Seemingly innocuous shades, especially when used for backgrounds, can kill other colours off if they are all of the same tone, reducing everything to muddiness. Most of what I have learned has come through trial and error, but it helps to look closely at fabrics and paintings to see how the artist has manipulated the shades.

The basis of freestyle (as opposed to geo-metric) needlepoint patterns is the art of making curves from straight lines. When I demonstrate, many people tell me that they find it difficult to decide at the edge of a petal, leaf or other curve, where to finish one colour and start the next. My response is to tell them not to worry about it and just keep stitching down the curve. You can always go back and add a stitch afterwards or stitch over one that still really bothers you when all is finished. But it is amazing how the eye adjusts, for how many pieces of work have you seen that really look stilted when finished? Filling in the background also pushes the stitches around a bit and softens the outlines. Many people return their completed needlepoint embroideries to me to have them made into cushions or stools; each is different, but I have never had one where the pattern has been spoiled, and am pleased when people make changes to suit their own colour scheme or incorporate stitch techniques that are appropriate. Fear is the biggest hurdle for many, but this can be overcome with a little freedom of the mind and fingers.

Silk design by James Leman, dated 1710 – the simple shapes and uncomplicated colouring are straightforward to translate into needlepoint.

scale patterns up or down so that they can be traced onto the canvas. After this, I sometimes paint the canvas, but usually I just get going and see what happens. I have no training in art, design, or needlework techniques and have learned most of what I know through trying things out and observing closely the work of others.

Running a needlepoint kit business, a large part of my job is to ensure that the designs we commission will be successful in kit form. I find myself having to stitch and experiment to achieve what the designer intends, for a design that is on paper will not always work on canvas. It was only a short step to design for myself; tracing shapes and images onto the canvas was a good way to begin, and is how I still set out most of my patterns.

Each design is introduced by showing the source material that inspired it, together with details about my approach when adapting the original for use on canvas and the way in which the colours were chosen. A flat photograph of each embroidered canvas is included so that you can see how effects have been achieved and how colours can work together in different contexts. You may observe that not all colours are pretty on their own but combine for an effect. These photographs also show how surface stitching can be used to add detail and interest to a flat finish. Charts do not show you this, and the idea of this book is to share my exploration of the V&A and the experience of working the pieces with the reader to give help, guidance and encouragement. You can use the shade palettes for your own work if the particular colour scheme suits your needs, as they are tried and tested, but do not be afraid to experiment with combinations of your own choosing. Some people will find the photographs a good enough guide to work from, but charts can be purchased by mail order if you prefer (see page 141).

Although there are detailed descriptions of a variety of stitch techniques as they arise in the text, the basic skills are covered in the section at the back of this book. Anyone who is new, or relatively new, to needlepoint should start by reading this section before embarking on any of the designs.

There are many uses for needlepoint, but purchased kits tend to be for cushions. Other items of furniture vary in size so much that it is difficult for manufacturers to produce kits that are sure to fit. This book provides an opportunity to show many different ways of using needlepoint – on chair seats and stools of all sizes, as bolsters

Facing page: A detail from the Fantasia panel, made to cover a nursing chair (see pages 60–65). Anna Maria Garthwaite's designs for woven silk provide a wealth of material for needlepoint patterns. As the flowers are imaginary one can be free with colours and take liberties with shapes.

and firescreens, and for simple upholstery. Most of the designs can be used in several ways and can easily be made to fit pieces of furniture of different sizes. It is not a difficult task to adapt designs to suit your needs, and suggestions for doing this are included throughout the text.

It is assumed that readers will include both beginners and experienced stitchers. I trust that the instructions will give you helpful guidance. However, the directions for making the stitched pieces into home furnishings assume a basic knowledge of sewing. Detailed instructions on joining piping cords, putting in zips and handling a sewing machine could fill a book on their own. Most people who sew enjoy sharing and showing off their skills to others; an hour of basic instruction from a friend should give you enough knowledge to tackle most of these projects, but perfect finishes are achieved through practice. Experiment first with spare scraps of fabric if you are unsure.

I have not attempted to do any in-depth research on the pieces chosen as the basis for these designs, but urge you if possible to visit the V&A to see and learn more. If the V&A is not accessible to you, your local museum or art gallery will undoubtedly house treasures that can be used as personal sources of inspiration. I have not set out to produce an historical tome, but rather to encourage needlepointers to have a go at creating their own patterns and to use the past as an inspiration for today. One can learn a great deal from copying something before taking the big step, and there is plenty of material here to work from. Prince Albert wanted us to use the Victoria and Albert Museum as a resource to help us to produce good designs. I hope this book will help you to do that.

COPTIC BIRD

It is amazing to think that the wool and linen tapestry that inspired the first needlepoint in the book was woven in Egypt some time in the fourth-to-fifth century. Although the original is badly frayed in many places, the stunningly bright colours have survived; astonishingly, one complete section of the fabric is intact, and it is from this that the design was taken.

The Copts are the native Egyptian Christians, who became theologically separated from mainstream Byzantine orthodoxy after the council of Chalcedon, in 451. Their art of this and the succeeding centuries is based on Egyptian ethnic motifs and colours, influenced by the Syrian and Persian cultures — a glorious mixture of naivety and sophistication, with the colours that are still to be found in Egyptian folk art. It is easy to understand how Coptic art spread far and wide, even — according to some — influencing the development of medieval Celtic art.

A friend who is an accomplished amateur watercolourist stitched this piece. She asked me to send her lots of colours so that she had a wide palette from which to choose to recreate the effect of the original. I envied her the task as I put together the bright turquoise, glowing greens and yellows, reds, blues and purples, all to be set off by the black background. I love working with bright colours, but have to restrain myself as so many people want softer shades for their homes. When I received the completed piece back, I was astonished to find that she had used nearly all the colours. Incorporating some quite subtle shading, she has brought this very old piece back to vibrant life. I was delighted and couldn't stop looking at it for days, but also felt that it would fit into many different settings because of its enduring quality. A dark navy background might soften the effect slightly, but I think the black is exciting.

I have shown the design on a soft footstool in this picture, but it could have many uses. By repeating the pattern in lines and then back to back as shown, it could either be adapted for a

Coptic Bird was taken from a piece of 4th-century Coptic Egyptian weaving. The Copts were famous for their weaving, and the twining leaves, grapes and birds were a recurring theme in their work.

This pattern can be widened by repeating it back to back (as shown here) as well as lengthened by continuing on as in the original (below).

cushion or elongated for a fender stool, something for which I am often asked. By changing the canvas gauge you can alter the size. On a very fine canvas, the design would be suitable for a bell pull (it is displayed that way up at the museum). Alternatively, it would make a fabulous carpet border on a big canvas, worked with two threads in the needle.

TO MAKE THE HASSOCK FOOTSTOOL

MATERIALS
$1\frac{1}{8}$yds (1m) of black elephant corduroy, 36in (90cm) wide
2yds (1.8m) of thick piping cord
14in (35cm) black zip
Polyester or feather filling
Matching thread

Use $\frac{5}{8}$in (1.5cm) seam allowances throughout.

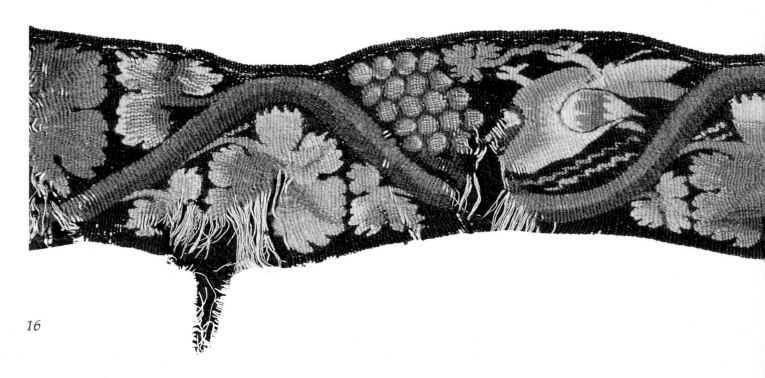

You can achieve a lovely corded effect in piping with this fabric if it is cut on the cross. Cut a strip 3in (7.5cm) wide, cutting from top left to bottom right of your fabric (in other words, diagonally across the centre of the fabric, leaving you with two large triangles). Cover your piping cord with this strip, folding it over the cord and using the zipper foot to stitch as close to the cord as possible. For the base: cut a rectangle 18 × 15in (38 × 46cm) lengthwise, along the grain of the fabric. The zip needs to be inserted into this panel, so cut it in half lengthwise: take the two pieces, put them with right sides together; stitch the seam 2in (5cm) at each end; press open, and then insert the zip in between. The finished panel should now measure $13\frac{1}{4}$ × 18in (34 × 46cm).

For the box edge, you need a piece 66in (1.65m) long and 7in (18cm) wide, with the grain of the fabric parallel with the short side. (You will need to cut two strips and sew them together to get sufficient length.)

Trim the canvas of your stitched needlepoint, leaving a margin of $\frac{5}{8}$in (1.5cm), and sew a panel of fabric to the top and bottom of the panel to make it the same size as the piece you have prepared for the base.

Baste the piping cord to this top piece. Machine around, again using the zipper foot and pushing up close to the piping cord. Baste the long piece of fabric to the piped top to make the

The Coptic Bird needlepoint panel is here made into a hassock, or footstool.

box edge. The right sides of the long piece of fabric and the top of the hassock should be together, with the piping in between. Machine this all the way around to make the piped top and box edge. The resulting short open seam is sewn up by hand. Turn the hassock inside out and, with right sides together, baste the bottom panel to the bottom edge of the box edge. Machine in place, remembering to leave the zip undone. Turn out the right way; fill tightly with feather or fibre pad, and close.

Coptic weaving from the 4th or 5th centuries — this sample is on display in the V&A museum, and well worth a visit to appreciate the detail and the glorious colours, which are much brighter than this picture suggests.

COPTIC BIRD

FINISHED STITCHED AREA
16¾ × 7in (42.5 × 17.5cm)

STITCH
Tent stitch (basketweave) or half cross stitch

MATERIALS
23 × 13in (58 × 33cm) of interlock canvas,
12 holes per inch (2.5cm)
Size 20 tapestry needle

ROWAN NEEDLEPOINT WOOL

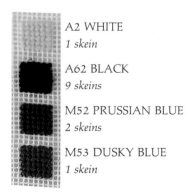

A2 WHITE
1 skein

A62 BLACK
9 skeins

M52 PRUSSIAN BLUE
2 skeins

M53 DUSKY BLUE
1 skein

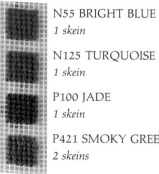

N55 BRIGHT BLUE
1 skein

N125 TURQUOISE BL

1 skein

P100 JADE
1 skein

P421 SMOKY GREEN
2 skeins

V75 SPRING GREEN
1 skein

V32 PALE GREENY YELLOW
1 skein

E79 PEACH
1 skein

V605 MID-GREEN
1 skein

E402 TANGERINE
1 skein

B5 PALE GOLD
1 skein

B152 GOLD
1 skein

V31 YELLOW
1 skein

G46 MAGENTA
1 skein

F45 RUST RED
1 skein

L137 LAVENDER
1 skein

THE OXBURGH HANGINGS

These curious hangings were stitched by Bess of Hardwick, and by Mary Queen of Scots during her imprisonment by her cousin Queen Elizabeth I in the late sixteenth century. Bess's husband of the time, the Earl of Salisbury, was responsible for keeping Mary prisoner, and it seems the two formidable women became friends. One of Mary's first requests was for 'an imbroiderer to draw forth such work as she would be occupied about'. She is reported to have said that 'all that Day she wrought with hir Nydill, and the Diversitie of the colours made the worke seem less tedious.' It must certainly have helped to pass the time. Most of the weird and wonderful creatures that feature in the Oxburgh hangings were copied directly from a scientific book called *Icones Animalium* by Conrad Gesner, published in Zurich in 1560.

How the ladies came across this unlikely title is not recorded; the animals seem a strange choice for a queen to stitch, and it is hard to imagine either Mary or Bess, who married four times and made a personal fortune from dealing in coal, lead and land, as keen needlewomen. Did Mary, with her French mother in mind, stitch A Frogge, while Bess – never outsmarted in a business deal – smilingly worked at Crocodil? Whatever impulse brought these strange embroideries into being, I love them for their oddity, and the funny spellings of the names. In fact, I have become devoted to them. Other motifs are ciphers and monographs relating to the lives of the two women who stitched them.

The panels were worked in cross stitch in silk on linen canvas, originally applied to green velvet to make four wall hangings. At a later date, three were converted into bed curtains and one, the source of the panels shown in the V&A, was cut up to serve as a valance. The three complete hangings were returned to their original use and are now on display at Oxburgh Hall. The pieces of the fourth hanging are displayed at the V&A.

Facing page: Crocodil and A. Frogge have been reworked, but other animals from the hangings would be equally suitable.

Hexagonal panel – the finished embroideries were appliquéd to green velvet to make large wall hangings.

A. Frogge – but there are two!

A. Frogge makes a jolly picture, and I think Crocodil would also, but I was tempted to try my hand at a version of the embroidery surround, as shown in the V&A picture, so mounted it onto a cushion. I cut the stitched piece out, leaving a canvas margin about ½in (12mm) deep, and then centred it on the velvet and basted it in position. Satin stitch in perle cotton thread covered this canvas margin; stem stitch was then added to both edges of the satin stitch to give the edge an even finish.

Velvet is difficult to work with so it is essential to hold the work in a frame to keep it flat during embroidery. I used two skeins of ecru cotton and a large sharp needle to stab through the fabric. The fragments of couched cord embroidery on the hanging led me to add some red lines of stem stitch, also in perle cotton thread, to relieve the plainness of the brown velvet.

Facing page: The reworked Crocodil from the Oxburgh hangings is mounted on a brown velvet cushion. Satin stitch, using perle embroidery cotton, covers the raw edges of the canvas.

CROCODIL

FINISHED STITCHED AREA
11½in (29cm) square

CUSHION SIZE
17in (43cm) square, excluding trim

STITCH
Tent stitch (basketweave) or half
cross stitch

MATERIALS
17in (43cm) square of interlock
canvas, 12 holes per inch (2.5cm)
Size 20 tapestry needle

ROWAN NEEDLEPOINT WOOL

Y3 PUTTY
3 skeins

K429 PALE DIRTY PINK
1 skein

Z64 SKY GREY
2 skeins

M422 GREY BLUE
1 skein

J427 SOFT BROWN
1 skein

J145 PINKY BROWN
2 skeins

X28 CHESTNUT
1 skein

W117 DARK BROWN
1 skein

B8 GOLD
1 skein

B5 PALE GOLD
1 skein

A. FROGGE

This was stitched by a friend some time ago, and hers are the initials on the right-hand side. There is no record of the wools originally used, and in selecting equivalents it has been necessary to allow slight variations in shade. The list of yarns begins with the background colours, starting from the top of the design, with M52, and working downward to W98.

FINISHED STITCHED AREA
Approximately 16in (40cm) in diameter

STITCH
Tent stitch (basketweave) or half cross stitch

MATERIALS
22in (55cm) square of interlock canvas, 14 holes per inch (2.5cm)
Size 20 tapestry needle

Previous page: A. Frogge, stitched as a picture. The whimsical frame was made with papier mâché, and the lily pads are painted cardboard. The modern frog — a woodcarving from Indonesia — is almost the same shape as the 16th-century version.

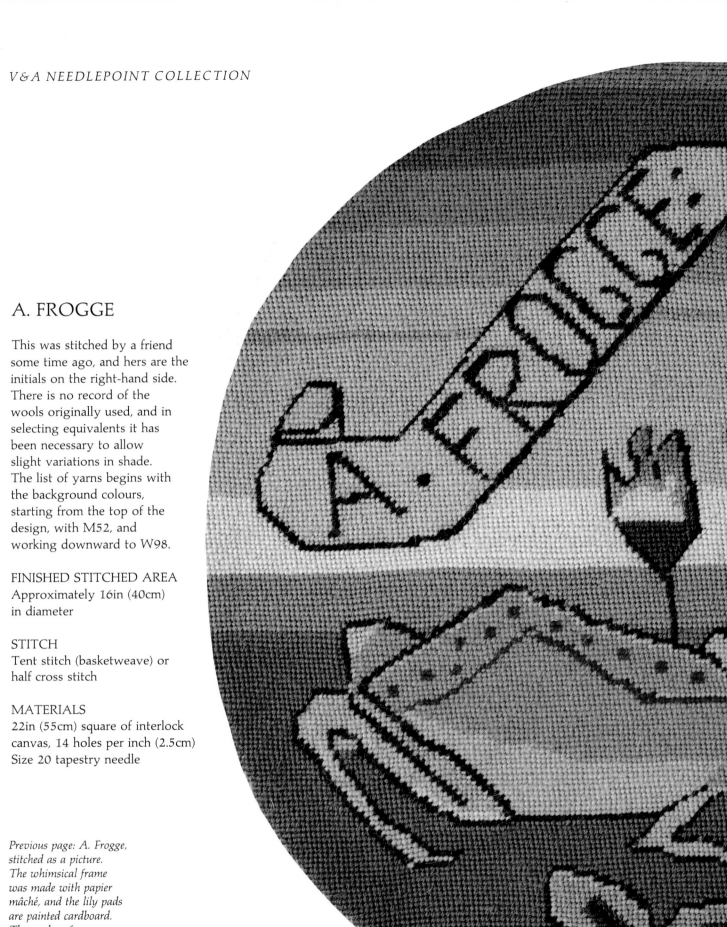

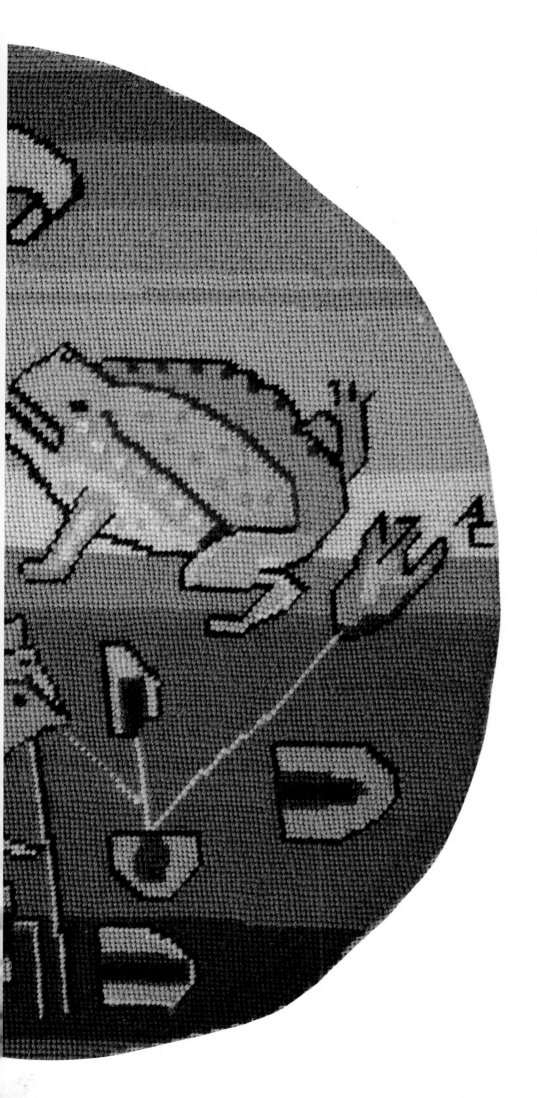

ROWAN NEEDLEPOINT WOOL

M52 PRUSSIAN BLUE
1 skein

M422 SKY GREY
1 skein

Z60 MID–GREY
2 skeins

Z64 DOVE GREY
3 skeins

Y58 PUTTY
2 skeins

P665 GREY MIST
3 skeins

W407 DARK OLIVE
5 skeins

W98 DARK BROWN
2 skeins

P417 LIGHT LEAF GREEN
2 skeins

P91 MIDDLE LEAF GREEN
1 skein

R606 DARK LEAF GREEN
1 skein

W150 FROG CANE
2 skeins

B5 FROG GOLD
2 skeins

B4 CREAM
1 skein

V619 SCROLL GREEN
2 skeins

X107 FROG CHESTNUT
1 skein

W117 OUTLINE BROWN
4 skeins

W. Bond, Still Life: Fruit, Bird and Dwarf Pear Tree, 1856.
National Gallery of Art, Washington

THE BRADFORD TABLE CARPET

The Bradford Table Carpet is one of the V&A's most exciting exhibits for needlepoint enthusiasts. An enormous table covering, it was embroidered in silk on a linen canvas, using mainly tent stitch, but with long stitch and stem stitch for some details. It took from 1605–1615 to embroider this design, in which there are approximately 400 stitches to the square inch. The figures are dressed in the fashion of the early 1600s, but the absence of heraldry suggests that the carpet was produced by a professional workshop for sale on the open market rather than as a specific commission. It formerly belonged to the earls of Bradford, at Castle Bromwich Hall.

The border appears to be a running commentary on country life, and shows people hunting, shooting, fishing, hawking, tending their domestic animals and growing fruit crops. Grand and simple houses, mills and farm buildings are all depicted with the wonderful disregard for scale that is characteristic of the embroideries of this era. The people are much too big for their homes, and the fruits on the trees are mammoth. Although the piece is English, many of the animals come from other parts of the world and some are not of this world at all. One wonders where the references came from and how the makers knew about leopards and other exotic species. The whole effect is of peace, harmony and prosperity. Officially, the design is alleged to depict the early stages of civilization and man's relationship with nature. Its charm is irresistible.

The carpet is on display at the V&A, but dim lighting has to be used to prevent fading, which makes it difficult to examine, especially as it is hung quite high up. When I got the colour transparencies I was amazed by the details and the strength of the colours.

Simple parts of the border were chosen as the basis for a couple of pieces in this book. The stool is mounted with a piece I have named Malakoff Castle. The fence reminds me of the trifle sponges that surround a Malakoff pudding. Much of this was copied stitch for stitch from the original, but in some places this was impractical.

Facing page: Little Nut Tree is from the border of the Bradford Table Carpet. Trees, animals, castles and cottages – all in needlepoint – provide a fund of exciting material for stitching. This tree is just a tiny detail.

The original tree from the Bradford Table Carpet – shows how very little had to be changed to make this into a picture (left).

*Previous page:
The border of the
Bradford Table
Carpet is a
continuous
narrative on
English country life
in the early 17th
century. This
section shows how
perspective and
scale are
disregarded, giving
the design a naive
charm that is
very appealing.*

Adjustments were made to the fence and the goat to fit them into the required shape; the end result is fairly close to the original work, though much larger in size. The seventeenth-century embroiders were working on a canvas that had 20 holes per inch (2.5cm) and we were working on 12 holes per inch. A fine canvas, such as a 16 holes per inch, embroidered in a silk thread, would bring one closer to the original.

I fell in love with the hazelnut tree, with its beautifully observed nut clusters and crazy paving trunk. The nuts are so big that you can only fit nine onto the whole tree. The bunny crept in at the last minute almost when I was not looking. I was afraid that it might not be possible to fit sufficient detail into so few stitches, but it worked the first time, so it had to stay. There are many other fruit trees in the carpet, and it would be fun to make them into a series, perhaps as chair seats.

The canvas had to be shaped slightly to fit this chair seat, so the front is four stitches wider on each side than the back. Measure the edges and mark, at each side of the canvas border, four evenly spaced places where you will increase by one stitch. The side strips were stitched separately and then sewn on afterwards, to provide a straight, firm edge. To make the end result strong enough to sit on, it is advisable to take it to an upholsterer, who will put a piece of strong canvas underneath and attach the ends firmly to the frame of your chair.

*Following page:
Malakoff Castle —
the fence reminds
me of the sponge
fingers around a
Malakoff pudding
— features a detail
from the border of
the Bradford Table
Carpet. Here, it is
used as a large
stool top.*

LITTLE NUT TREE

The size can be varied to fit your own chair by adding or subtracting from the background (see also page 135); the finished piece shown here measured 11 × 17in (28 × 43cm).

STITCHES

Tent stitch (basketweave) or half cross is used for the main embroidery, and the stitch illustrated on page 57 for the side strips.

MATERIALS

Interlock canvas, with 12 holes per inch (2.5cm), some 3in (7.5cm) larger all around than the finished embroidery; plus more for side strips, if required.
Size 20 tapestry needle

ROWAN NEEDLEPOINT WOOL

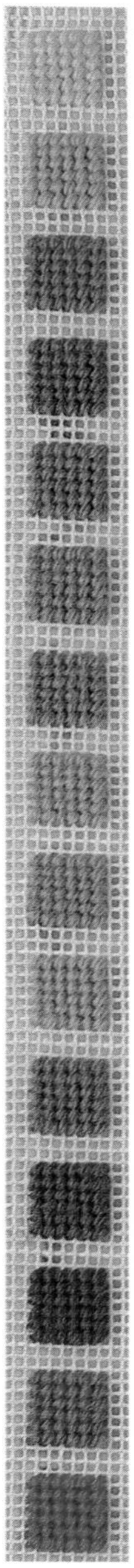

A2 WHITE
2 skeins

N47 PALE SKY BLUE
7 skeins

M52 PRUSSIAN BLUE
1 skein

P421 SMOKY GREEN
2 skeins

V605 MID-GREEN
3 skeins

V617 OLIVE
1 skein

V664 GREEN HAY
5 skeins

B5 PALE GOLD
2 skeins

B8 OLD GOLD
2 skeins

Y614 PALE BEIGE
5 skeins

Y82 LIGHT BROWN
2 skeins

J427 PINKY BROWN
2 skeins

X87 BROWN
2 skeins

J434 OLD ROSE
1 skein

J424 DEEP SALMON
1 thread

MALAKOFF CASTLE

FINISHED STITCHED AREA
22 × 18in (56 × 46cm)

STITCH
Tent stitch (basketweave) or half cross stitch

MATERIALS
28 × 24in (70 × 60cm) of interlock canvas,
12 holes per inch (2.5cm)
Size 20 tapestry needle

ROWAN NEEDLEPOINT WOOL

G435 CRIMSON *2 skeins*	V605 MID-GREEN *1 skein*
H659 PLUM BROWN *1 skein*	P418 SMOKY GREEN *1 skein*
J145 PINKY BROWN *1 skein*	X87 BROWN *6 skeins*
J411 DUSKY ROSE *1 skein*	E147 TOFFEE *2 skeins*
J148 DIRTY PINK *4 skeins*	E104 AMBER *6 skeins*
E20 PEACH *1 skein*	M88 SLATE BLUE *1 skein*
E79 PALE PEACH *1 skein*	M111 BLUE *4 skeins*
E401 EVEN PALER PEACH *5 skeins*	Z64 PALE GREY *3 skeins*
B4 PALE STRAW *10 skeins*	A2 WHITE *1 skein*
B5 PALE GOLD *6 skeins*	
V617 PALE OLIVE *3 skeins*	
V105 OLIVE *5 skeins*	

LONG-STITCH CHAIR SEAT

It was the stained glass gallery at the V&A that inspired this piece. Stained glass is made with lead outlines, filled in with solid blocks of colour, allowing each shade to stand alone as well as forming an important element of the whole design. Needlepoint wool has a dense quality that suits this medium, and I wanted to include a pattern in long stitch here to show off the colours in their own right, and also to create a design that would be much easier to stitch than the rather complicated Bargello patterns, made with vertical zigzag patterns in long stitch, which require a lot of counting. I have been asked by friends to help them out when they have embroidered long rows of counted stitches and got lost half way through. When relaxing in the evening with a piece of needlework, few of us want to be tested in this way.

Long-stitch patterns are attractive in themselves and quick to complete. They are rarely available printed on the canvas, as exact patterns do not print well on an inexact fabric. The loose weave of canvas means that the warp and the weft are rarely straight or square, and the size of the holes on the canvas varies slightly. Attempts to print straight lines and geometric patterns on this medium can lead to disappointment.

However, long-stitch patterns need not rely on endless counting if a simple outline shape is created and then repeated across the canvas. Having done this, you can then fill in the shapes with lots of colours. Here, I have made a shape that is like a little house and have repeated it across the first row. For the next row, I turned the shape upside down. The new shapes that this created between the rows were a bonus, and did not have to be thought about at all, but gave an opportunity for using yet another colour.

It is a good idea to repeat your colour choices every three or four rows to give the piece a balance and the impression that it has been planned. I used over 30 colours here, and felt that this was more than enough for the eye to deal with. Some people may find them too bright for living rooms, but passing places, such as hallways, can take strong spots of colour without wearying the eye. In any event, this design would not wear well as a dining chair— shorter stitches and a finer canvas would add strength, but the stitches used here are too long and loose. When working in long stitch, you need to be sure that the wool will cover the canvas sufficiently well, so for this pattern I chose a canvas with 14 holes per inch (2.5cm), rather than the 12 holes per inch gauge that I use most frequently. If you choose a larger gauge, it is advisable to use two strands of wool in the needle. Stitch a small sample to ensure that the mix of canvas and wool suits your needs.

It is essential to use a frame for this work, because the canvas often gets slightly pulled when you make long stitches. This may be imperceptible as you are working, but the finished piece will not lie flat unless the stitches are even, which is difficult to achieve with hand-held work.

Facing page: Bright colours may be difficult to place in a sitting room, but can cheer up a dark hallway or landing. It is liberating to stitch these strong colours, using long stitches that cover the canvas quickly.

LONG-STITCH CHAIR SEAT

For each shape:
outline colour – 30in (75cm)
filling colour – 30in (75cm)

The finished chair seat shown here measured 24in (60cm) across at the widest point, and 22in (56cm) in depth, but these measurements can be adjusted by adding or subtracting rows of pattern to fit your own chair (see also page 135). This project offers a chance to invent your own colour scheme, and can be made to almost any dimensions, so rather than give skein quantities, we have listed the length of yarn used for each shape.

STITCH
Long stitch

MATERIALS
Interlock canvas, 14 holes per inch (2.5cm), some 3in (7.5cm) larger all around than the finished embroidery.
Size 20 tapestry needle

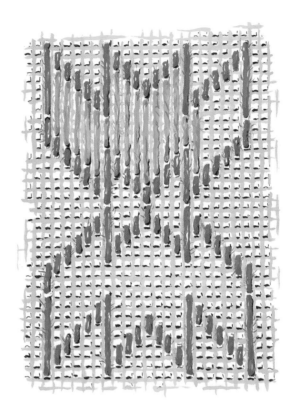

ROWAN NEEDLEPOINT WOOL

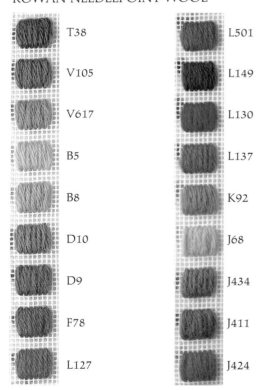

T38	L501	J145	P421
V105	L149	Z61	P89
V617	L130	M88	P90
B5	L137	M52	N141
B8	K92	M53	M413
D10	J68	M151	Y58
D9	J434	M54	H70
F78	J411	P655	G46
L127	J424	P91	G43

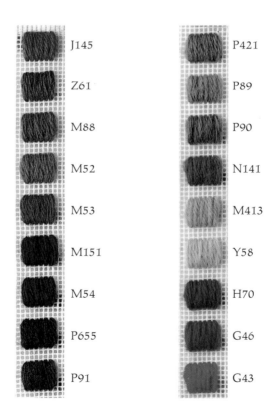

INDIAN TRELLIS

I visited India a couple of years ago and fell in love with it. Indians decorate everything, and the resulting beauty that is brought even to utilitarian objects and to humble shops and buildings is extraordinary. Having fallen under the spell, I was immediately drawn to the V&A Indian Collection. The drawings of architectural details were acquired when, as a result of the Great Exhibition in London in 1851, people started to become aware of the great wealth of Indian arts and crafts.

I love the patterns for screens that seem to bend the eyes in different directions. They remind me of the Amber Palace outside Jaipur, where such intricately carved screens are used instead of window glass, allowing gentle breezes to waft through the rooms. Transferring this fascinating geometric pattern to canvas was a challenge, but its very dark background enabled the design to retain some of the depth of the original water colour. I found it was best not to try to make the pattern 'perfect', with each hexagon having the same stitch formation as the last – it looked much more alive when they were not exact copies. In fact the hexagons in the

drawings themselves are not all exactly the same size, and were probably drawn by eye rather than by rule.

Flowers were of key importance in the development of Mughal architectural design. Sometimes, rosettes are inserted into the overall

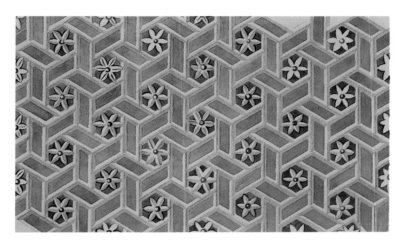

plan and set into their own spaces, as in the hexagons of this pattern. In other patterns, relating to carpet design or manuscript illustration, flowers are an integral part. Both uses were adopted to make this stool and the colours are chosen from the Indian miniature paintings, with those deep, strong pastels and washes of turquoise in the greens, that are so evocative of India.

For the chair seat, I changed the colours, but am not convinced that they are an improvement. If I were to stitch this design again I might choose the same colours for the trellis itself, but use something gentler for the flowers. It is all a matter of personal taste and what suits your home.

This Indian architectural design, probably intended for a carved screen, is executed in watercolour. It appears to have been done freehand rather than measured out exactly, and the result is much prettier than a mathematically perfect one would have been. There is a lesson for needlepointers here!

45

INDIAN TRELLIS
CHAIR SEAT

The finished stitched area of the chair seat shown here measured 24in (60cm) across at the widest point, and 23in (59cm) in depth, but these measurements can be adjusted by adding or subtracting background to fit your own chair (see also page 135). As chairs vary in size and different colour combinations have been used to illustrate a variety of choices of background, it is impossible to give a yarn count that will be useful. You will need approximately 80in (2m) of yarn to cover a square inch (2.5cm).

To stitch the flowers in the centre you will need two skeins of each flower colour and three skeins each of the greens for the leaves.

STITCH
Cross stitch

MATERIALS
Interlock canvas, 10 holes per inch (2.5cm), some 3in (7.5cm) larger all around than the finished embroidery.
Size 18 tapestry needle

ROWAN NEEDLEPOINT WOOL

H659 PLUM BROWN
centre background

H85 ROSE MADDER
hexagon background

F24 AMBER
rosettes

J424 SALMON
rosettes

J148 DUSTY PINK
rosettes and flowers

J83 PALE PINK
rosettes and flowers

Y58 STONE
hexagons

B84 PALE STRAW
hexagons

B116 YELLOW
flowers

B8 OLD GOLD
flowers

V664 PALE OLIVE
rosettes and flowers

P418 SMOKY GREEN
leaves

P430 GREEN
leaves

M88 SLATE BLUE
hexagon outline

M52 PRUSSIAN BLUE
rosettes and flowers

M123 DUCK EGG BLUE
rosettes and flowers

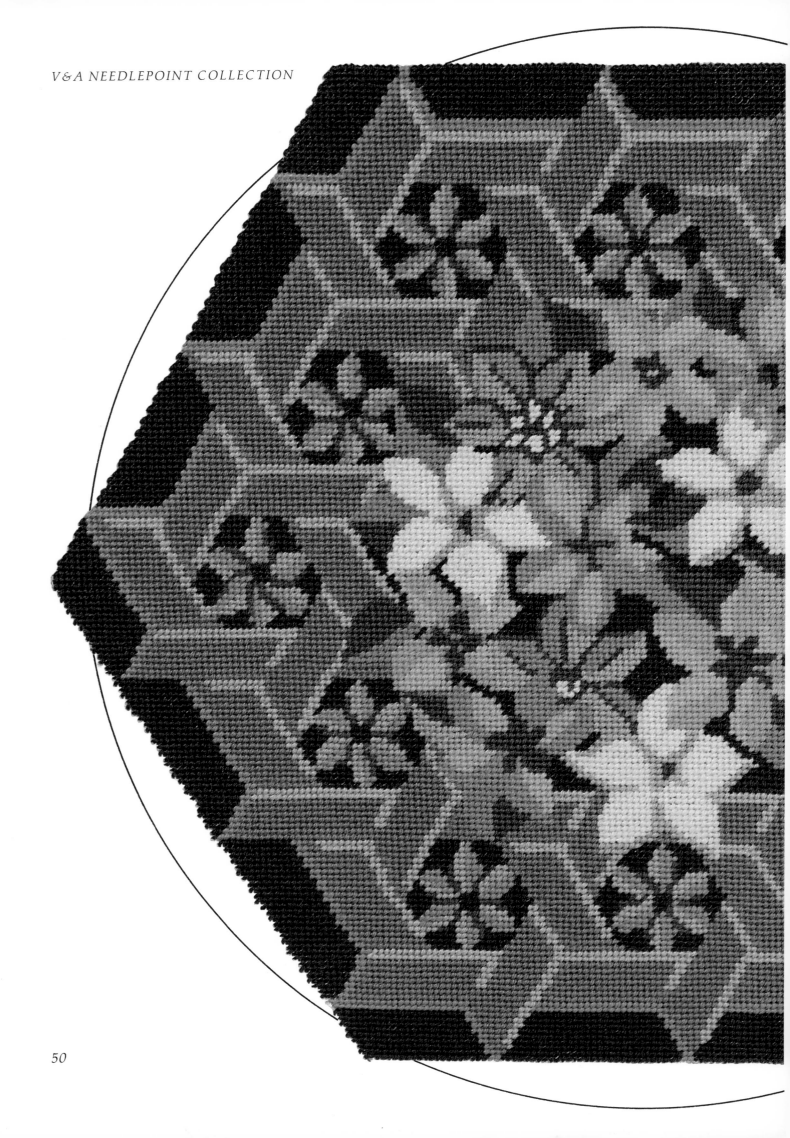

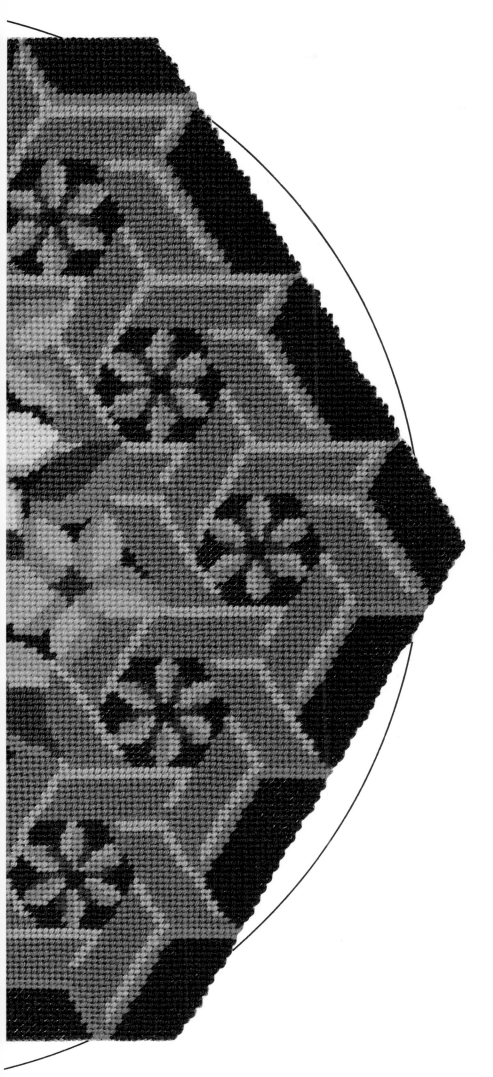

INDIAN TRELLIS STOOL

FINISHED STITCHED AREA
15in (38cm) in diameter, this pattern will also fit a circular stool

STITCH
Tent stitch (basketweave) or half cross stitch

MATERIALS
21in (53cm) square of interlock canvas, 12 holes per inch (2.5cm)
Size 20 tapestry needle

ROWAN NEEDLEPOINT WOOL

Y614 PALE BEIGE
4 skeins

Y82 BEIGE
6 skeins

Z60 GREY
4 skeins

Z65 DARK GREY
8 skeins

M52 PRUSSIAN BLUE
2 skeins

N123 DUCK EGG BLUE
2 skeins

P416 PALE MINT
2 skeins

J68 PINK
1 skein

J410 ROSE PINK
1 skein

E20 APRICOT
1 skein

E103 PALE APRICOT
1 skein

B131 YELLOW
1 skein

V30 PALE LEMON
1 skein

S433 MINT
2 skeins

P100 DARK JADE
2 skeins

EIGHTEENTH-CENTURY SILK DESIGNS

The V&A owns by far the most important and extensive collection of eighteenth-century silk designs in the world. Some are bound, some loose, and some are actual fabric samples in pattern books. Most of these were produced for the European fashion market and for export to the American colonies. It was not only the women who wanted flowered silks for their dresses; the most elaborate and brocaded designs were often intended for the men's jackets and waistcoats, using gold and silver thread on top of fabulous coloured silks.

A major exhibition of these collections was mounted at the V&A in 1990, and was called 'Flowered Silks: A Nobel Manufacture of the Eighteenth Century'. The whole exhibition made a lasting impression on me, and two designers remained strongly in my mind – James Leman, whose colours and clearly defined floral motifs have an extraordinary freshness and could have been designed today, and Anna Maria Garthwaite, the master of invented flowers. Her shapes are from fantasy land and great fun to stitch, while her colours are soft and rich. When I started work on this book, I immediately went in search of examples of their work from which I might draw some ideas for needlepoint. To my delight, further research revealed that both were rather unusual people.

James Leman was a manufacturer as well as a designer, which was uncommon. His family originally came from Amsterdam, but his father settled in Canterbury, England, after they had suffered persecution as Huguenots. Anna Maria Garthwaite was a freelance designer, apparently untrained but with an amazing grasp of the design requirements for working with silk looms. She was prolific, producing up to 80 designs in a single year. Silk weaving was an important industry in England at this time, much of it undertaken in workshops scattered around Spitalfields in London, and also in Canterbury.

Part of a silk weaving design by James Leman (1710); the V&A have recently acquired a volume of his glorious designs, which draw on exotic architectural and floral references. The early Leman designs were rich and fantastic and were intended for weaving that included real gold and silver thread.

Detail from a silk design (dated 1707) by Christopher Baudonin, who supplied designs to the Leman weaving workshop. Natalie Rothstein, a curator at the V&A, describes his work as 'delicate, accomplished and, of course, absolutely fashionable'.

CANDLE FIRESCREEN

The design on which the firescreen is based comes from a volume of 97 drawings, mostly by James Leman, which belonged to Vanners Silks until 1991, when they were purchased by the V&A. Vanners still exist; their original premises were in Spitalfields, but they are now based outside London, in Sudbury, and are part of a larger group of companies.

I enjoyed working on this design enormously, and adhered fairly closely to the original, because there was little need to change things. I had to add more colours because of the solid effect that stitched needlepoint creates. Watercolour contains an enormous amount of variation and shading in each brush stroke which is not necessarily apparent, but nevertheless gives a light touch. When you change this for solid colour, as in a needlepoint, the effect is deadening, but adding more shades here seems to have solved the problem. It was important to handle these additions with care, using paler and darker shades of existing colours where possible, to retain the character of the piece. However, the candles needed emphasis and were so appealing that I was not afraid to accentuate them with a definite green.

I designed this firescreen in December, and I cannot help feeling that it has a Christmas atmosphere. I would like to try it in traditional Christmas colours, with touches of gold thread in the candle flames.

These shapes and colours appear so modern that it is difficult to believe they were originally conceived in 1710. Large areas of single colours make a refreshing change after working very detailed flowers and intricately shaded leaves. It was also fun to use different stitches and to

Previous page: The Candle Firescreen is an almost direct lift from James Leman's silk design. A little more colour was needed to achieve an interesting effect in wool, and a variety of stitches has been used to add interest to large areas of single colour.

experiment with surface embroidery to make the little trees. Because one side is the mirror image of the other, I thought it would be interesting to take this symmetry into the stitching. If you look carefully at the flat photograph, you will see that on the left-hand side the stitches run from top left to bottom right, and on the right-hand side they run in the more usual direction of top right to bottom left. If you want to do this, turn the work clockwise by 90 degrees so that you are holding it sideways on. Stitch normally, from top right to bottom left, as you see it. When you turn it upright, you will see that the stitches run backwards, as required. If your canvases distort badly when you stitch, I advise you *not* to do this as you will find that the centre of the work will go out of shape (see pages 132–3 for advice on reducing distortion).

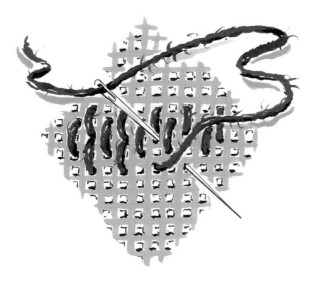

Most of the cream background is stitched in a version of Gobelin, consisting of straight up and down stitches over two threads of canvas. Alternate rows lock together, resembling narrow brickwork if you turn the needlepoint on its side.

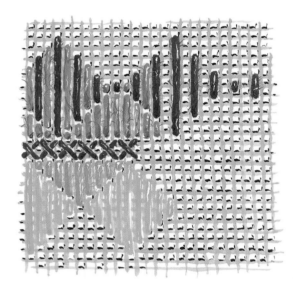

The long stitches shown above are surrounded by lines of cross stitch over two threads of canvas. The diagram also shows the configuration of the long stitches. The stitch used for the candles is illustrated below.

The little trees are embroidered freestyle on

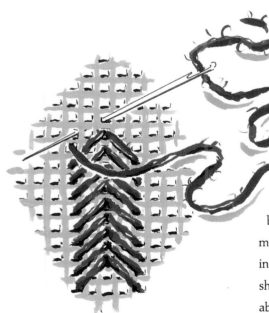

the surface of the stitching. Start at the top with a vertical stitch for the point and then work downwards from side to side. Do not worry

about uneveness, as the french knots (see page 133) will hide the joins. I have used many french knots here. Some details in the original were too difficult to stitch successfully, but something was needed in their place. The knots are worth experimenting with, as they are easily formed and quick to undo if they look wrong.

ORDER OF STITCHING

I generally start at the centre of a design and work outward, but the order of stitching must ultimately depend upon the pattern. Backgrounds should always be filled in last as you want to be free to ensure that your shapes and curves are to your satisfaction before you lock them in. If the background is worked in a different stitch to the rest of the design, this is even more important, as you will have to adjust the stitch to fit the pattern in places.

CHANGING THE SIZE TO FIT YOUR FIRESCREEN

The pattern can be made taller by changing the shape of the brown wiggly line above the longest candle and then adding background to fit.

To make it shorter, change the height of the candles and adjust the brown wiggly line to make it a little lower. If more is needed, take it off the bottom of the pattern, but keep the two floral motifs at the bottom corners. Move these up an inch (2.5cm) and leave out the bottom strap shape in long stitch, which lies immediately above this motif.

To make the design wider, add background and continue the shapes that currently end with the edge. To square off the top, simply add more background.

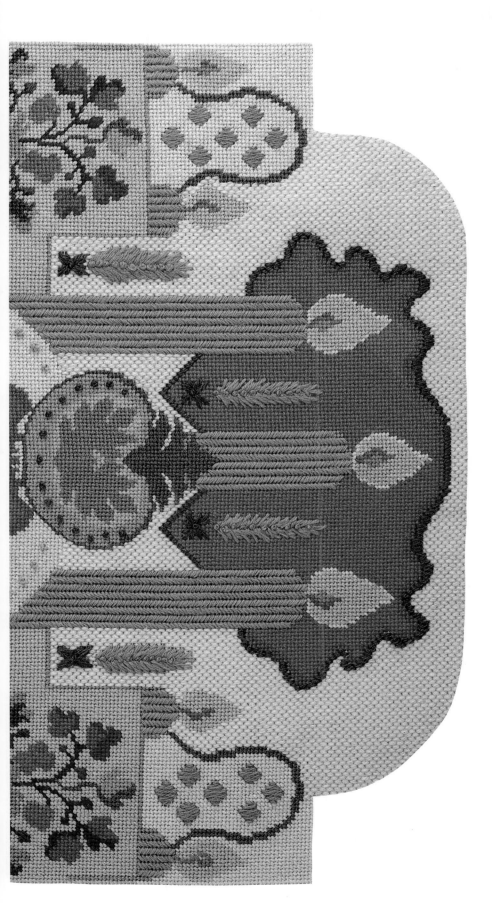

CANDLE FIRESCREEN

FINISHED STITCHED AREA
The screen shown here measures $24\frac{3}{4} \times 18\frac{1}{2}$in
(63×47cm); for advice on altering the
dimensions, see page 57.

STITCHES
Tent stitch (basketweave) or half cross stitch,
Gobelin, herringbone, french knots, long stitch,
cross stitch and surface embroidery in long stitch

MATERIALS
Interlock canvas, 12 holes per inch (2.5cm),
3in (7.5cm) larger all around than the finished
embroidery
Size 20 tapestry needle

ROWAN NEEDLEPOINT WOOL

F78 AMBER
3 skeins

E20 PEACH
4 skeins

E79 PALE PEACH
7 skeins

E104 BUTTERSCOTCH
5 skeins

B5 PALE GOLD
3 skeins

B4 CREAM
18 skeins

M52 PRUSSIAN BLUE
4 skeins

N63 SKY BLUE
3 skeins

V605 MID-GREEN
7 skeins

W139 POND GREEN
4 skeins

D10 OLD GOLD
4 skeins

H132 WINE RED
2 skeins

J424 BRIGHT PINK
7 skeins

FANTASIA CHAIR

I wish Anna Maria Garthwaite were alive today. Not only would she make an exciting needlepoint designer but I would love to know more about her. I would love to ask her why she worked so unceasingly, and how she learned her trade without the normal apprenticeship. Her work demonstrates a detailed knowledge of the design requirements for weaving. For a woman to be so successful in this male-dominated world, especially as a freelance designer, was certainly unusual. Working closely with her designs, I wonder where she derived her inspiration from, so inventive and fantastic are the flowers and garlands. The difficulty for me was to choose, from the hundreds of patterns that she left behind, just four examples on which to base some pieces for this collection.

One project was to cover a little fireside or nursing chair, using the pattern of fantasy flowers and shapes shown opposite. Anna Maria's design was probably intended for a brocaded silk, and there are only slight touches of colour, so I had a free hand to choose my own. This was the first piece on which I worked for this book, and it was also the first time that I had experienced the joy of designing without all the limitations imposed by kits, where one must consider the problems of printing on canvas and the expense of using lots of colours. The freedom simply to pick up another shade in order to add a touch of light or shadow was exhilarating. When I had finished, however, I was surprised that I had used only 24 colours and not the 50 or so that it felt like. As one of the aims of this book is to encourage people to experiment with design, and certainly to make colour changes — as necessary — to existing schemes, it may be helpful to share my experience in developing this design. What I learned was that you can lose your way and end up with an unbalanced piece if you are not practised in the use of a large number of shades. It is better to use a restricted palette when planning the colours for the dominant features in the pattern, and only let go on the details. I always make a shade card as I go along so that I don't get lost, and know which numbers to select, especially if the light is not good.

Starting with acquamarine and green, I picked out shades close to these colours to achieve a soft and graduated result. Moving in one direction from pink, I ran into pale mauves, and going in the other direction from pink were apricot colours. The background had to be a strong contrast. Anna Maria's was brown and I tried to find a wool that matched the shade. However, the solidity of the result made it look dreary — there is so much light and shadow in the watercolour that it is not achievable in wool. The important thing was to set the flower colours off to their best advantage, while keeping in the spirit of the original. A dark, aubergine brown looked good, but might have become overwhelming. To offset this, and to give the piece a used look appropriate to the antique chair, I put a band of dark, dusty purple down the centre. It is almost indiscernible, but gave the effect I sought.

This chair was a junk shop find that needed a new cover, so here was a perfect opportunity. The dimensions could, however, fit a fender stool, and the length or width could easily be adjusted by repeating the pattern or adding more background.

Facing page: This silk design was created by Anna Maria Garthwaite (in 1741). Anna Maria was described as one of three English designers 'who attempted to introduce the principles of painting into the loom'. She was already interested in natural forms before botanical styles became fashionable in the 1740s.

Following page: Fantasia Chair is taken from a silk weaving design by Anna Maria Garthwaite (see page 60). Her fantastic flowers are a gift for needlepoint; indeed, several of her early designs are thought to be for professional embroidery.

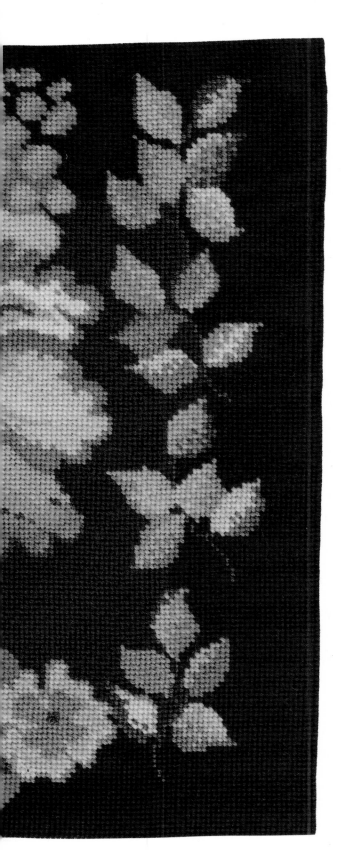

FANTASIA CHAIR

The panel measures approximately 38 × 13¼in (97 × 34cm), but it was made wider in the middle to allow the upholsterer to accommodate the bend without stretching the canvas too tightly. The pattern repeat measures 14½in (37cm), and the twining leaves are added to the top and bottom to finish the design.

STITCHES
Tent stitch (basketweave) or half cross stitch, and french knots

MATERIALS
Interlock canvas, 12 holes per inch, 3in (7.5cm) larger all around than the finished embroidery
Size 20 tapestry needle

ROWAN NEEDLEPOINT WOOL

H659 PLUM BROWN *60in (1.5m) per 1in (2.5cm) square*		**V30 PALE LEMON** *2 skeins*	
L652 DARK PURPLE *60in (1.5m) per 1in (2.5cm) square*		**V619 STONE** *2 skeins*	
L121 LILAC *1 skein*		**V617 PALE OLIVE** *1 skein*	
K128 PINKY MAUVE *1 skein*		**V135 PALE GREEN** *1 skein*	
K425 DIRTY PINK *1 skein*		**V605 MID-GREEN** *2 skeins*	
K429 PALE DIRTY PINK *1 skein*		**P418 SMOKY GREEN** *2 skeins*	
J68 PINK *2 skeins*		**P665 GREY MIST** *1 skein*	
J83 PALE PEACH *2 skeins*		**N48 SKY BLUE** *1 skein*	
E20 APRICOT *1 skein*		**N123 DUCK EGG BLUE** *1 skein*	
E79 PALE APRICOT *1 skein*		**N122 ACQUAMARINE** *2 skeins*	
E401 PALER APRICOT *2 skeins*		**M49 LIGHT BLUE** *2 skeins*	
B84 CREAM *1 skein*		**P90 JADE** *1 skein*	

FANTASIA CUSHION

Using the pattern for the flowers from the Fantasia Chair, but a very different gauge canvas (7 holes to the inch), and two strands of wool threaded on the needle, I developed a design that can be a cushion, stool top, chair back or what you will. The more modern leaves were added to change the mood to one suited to the scale of the canvas. I have always been daunted by this big canvas, and afraid that the designs would look stilted and the lines jagged. I decided, therefore, to copy something that had already proved successful on a small scale, and it seemed to work. This gave me the confidence to stitch the leaves and not worry about the seemingly huge jumps that have to be made from one stitch to the next when trying to create a curve.

There are some minor difficulties in using two threads on the needle. When you pull the wool through, the threads do not always pull at the same rate and so have to be evened up when you have finished the stitch. The longer the threads used, the more of a problem this becomes; shorter lengths are much easier to work with, but of course you have to stop and start more often.

Having mastered the technique and got over the fears, I enjoyed the sensation of the scale and the speed with which one could cover the canvas. This encouraged me to have a second try, and I thought the rose in Double Damask (page 00) would be lovely in a big version. First, I had an enlarged colour photocopy made to see if it would work. I then cut out the flower, glued it to a clean sheet of paper, and painted the leaves before committing myself to canvas. Large gauge canvas makes a refreshing change. After this jumbo scale, my usual 12 holes to the inch gauge felt tiny in comparison.

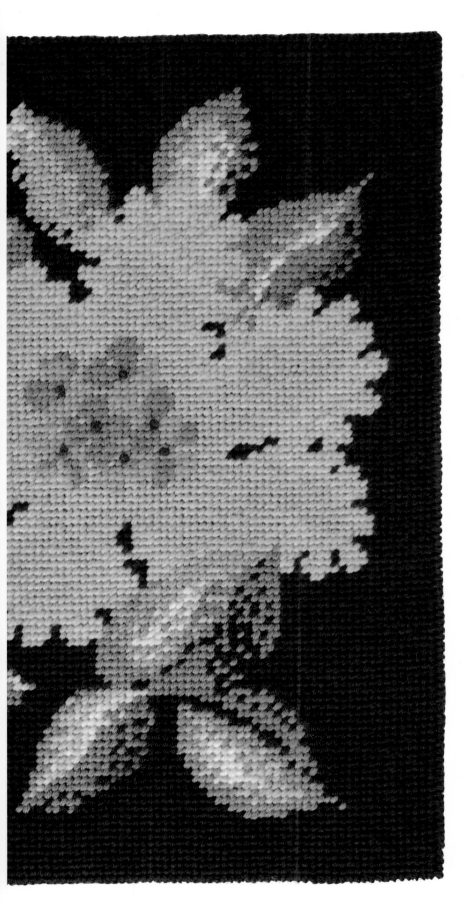

FANTASIA CUSHION

FINISHED STITCHED AREA
$19\frac{1}{2} \times 16$in (50×40.5cm)

STITCHES
Tent stitch (basketweave) was used, with french knots; half cross would give too thin a finish on this large-scale canvas. Use two threads in the needle throughout.

MATERIALS
24×20in (60×50cm) of interlock canvas, 7 holes per inch (2.5cm)
Size 16 tapestry needle

ROWAN NEEDLEPOINT WOOL

H659 PLUM BROWN
20 skeins

L121 LILAC
1 skein

K425 DIRTY PINK
3 skeins

J68 PINK
4 skeins

E79 PEACH
3 skeins

E401 PALEST PEACH
3 skeins

R606 DARK GREEN
3 skeins

V605 MID-GREEN
2 skeins

V664 PALE OLIVE
3 skeins

V619 STONE
3 skeins

V30 PALE LEMON
1 skein

P90 JADE
1 skein

N122 ACQUAMARINE
1 skein

N123 DUCK EGG BLUE
1 skein

Seen here is the original pattern from which the Antique Bolster design was taken. To avoid a striped effect, a slight re-distribution of colours was needed when adapting it for needlepoint.

ANTIQUE BOLSTER

When designing a bolster you have to think of the pattern as one continuous form that goes around and around. Anna Maria Garthwaite's repeating patterns are ideal, and once again my local photocopying shop was extremely helpful and produced a blow-up of my tracing that fitted the circumference of the bolster cushion perfectly.

This was taken from a design for a tobine (warp-patterned silk). As you can see from the illustration, Anna Maria's design includes subtly shaded stripes to accommodate the loom. This works with silks, where there is a lot of reflection off the cloth, reducing the starkness of the joins in the colours. In wool, this would look stiff rather than shaded, so I took the basis of her palette but distributed it differently. The colours of the flowers make quite strong statements, and the scarlet touches bring out the richness of the greens. A powdery background as needed to show these off to their best advantage while softening the overall effect.

Previous page: The Antique Bolster is from the above silk weaving design by Anna Maria Garthwaite (dated 1741). The repeat lends itself to a bolster, for which the pattern needs to be continuous.

Bolsters need borders, but I felt that it would have been presumptuous to add anything to what seemed a perfect pattern. The answer was to take a feature from the pattern, rather than creating something new, and repeat it right around the edge. I love this posy of flowers and leaves, and four posies fitted perfectly along each edge. The shaded check pattern underneath I took from another damask silk, using it simply to emphasize its purpose as a border, but in retrospect I wish I had added another row of squares to each side. I would have liked to have used this motif again to make ends for the bolster, and have painted a piece of canvas to show my intention. Time did not allow me to make these adjustments, but the idea is there for anyone to adopt. To make the ends, copy the little flowers and then put in the check squares behind up to a diameter of 7in (18cm).

Having talked exclusively about bolsters, I should also point out that this would serve equally well as a large stool top, and the central pattern would fit a long, narrow fender stool if the border were omitted.

MAKING THE BOLSTER

If you wish to make a bolster, it is essential that the finished needlepoint is carefully stretched (see page 134), to ease out any distortion.

MATERIALS

10in (25cm) of fabric, 36in (90cm) wide
Two large buttons from a covering kit,
$1\frac{1}{2}$in (4cm) in diameter
Bolster pad 20in (50cm) long and 7in (18cm) in diameter (see page 141 for Rowan suppliers), *or* a role of polyester batting
Matching thread

Use $\frac{1}{2}$in (1.5cm) seam allowances throughout. Trim the stitched canvas leaving a margin of $\frac{1}{2}$in (1.5cm). Cut the fabric lengthwise in half to make two strips 5 × 24ins (13 × 61cm). With right sides together, machine these two strips to the longest sides of your stitched canvas. Run two lines of gathering thread along the raw edges at each end. Fold the resulting piece in two, wrong side out, with the fabric strips at each end. Baste and sew the raw edges together to make a long tube. Turn the bolster right side out; insert the bolster pad, and pull up the gathering threads as tightly as possible.

Use the spare fabric to cover your buttons, according to the kit instructions. Sew them on each end of the bolster to cover the gathered raw ends.

If you have chosen to make needlepoint ends for your bolster, make it up as described above, but without the fabric strips. When your bolster pad is in the tube, sew the needlepoint ends in place, using your tapestry needle and wool. Strips of braid at each end will help to cover any unevenness in the sewing.

A detail of the Antique Bolster — the unstitched canvas marked with a circle and posy of flowers, on the left, is a suggestion for making needlepoint ends for the bolster.

ANTIQUE BOLSTER

FINISHED STITCHED AREA
$22\frac{1}{2} \times 18$in (57×46cm), to make a bolster 18in (46cm) long and 7in (18cm) in diameter

STITCH
Tent stitch (basketweave) or half cross stitch

MATERIALS
$28\frac{1}{2} \times 24$in (71×60cm) of interlock canvas, 12 holes per inch (2.5cm)
Size 20 tapestry needle

ROWAN NEEDLEPOINT

A2 WHITE
5 skeins

K429 PALE PINKY MAUVE
5 skeins

J69 DUSTY PINK
4 skeins

H70 DEEP ROSE
4 skeins

H85 MAROON
2 skeins

G42 BRIGHT RED
1 skein

B5 PALE GOLD
1 skein

B8 GOLD
1 skein

D10 OLD GOLD
1 skein

W407 POND GREEN
4 skeins

P418 SMOKY GREEN
5 skeins

P665 GREY MIST
32 skeins

P416 PALE MINT
6 skeins

LITTLE PINK FLOWER

Inspired by another delightful silk pattern by Anna Maria Garthwaite, I started out to make something really big. However, having com-

Detail from a silk weaving design by Anna Maria Garthwaite (dated 1742).

pleted the pink flower I was not sure where to go next. This was a lesson in what happens when you do not plan properly before starting. I nearly discarded the design altogether until someone

asked me to create a pattern for a photograph frame. I worked out a pattern for my friend and then tried it out on the pink flower. The pattern is much more complicated than it looks, and I did not count it correctly. When I got to the corners I had to cheat to make it fit, as you can see if you study the flat picture closely. Contrary to my usual advice that borders should be stitched last, it is wise to stitch this one first, and then put the design inside – it is easier to adjust the floral design than the geometric border pattern.

I have used a few surface stitches in the flower centre in an attempt to achieve the effect of Anna Maria's weaving lines. It is worth experimenting with these long stitches as they are easy to take out if they do not work. I also used the french knots to which I am so attached. The important thing is to control their size by holding the yarn tight (instructions are given at the back of this book).

Velvet surrounds for needlepoint have a quality that enhances the work every time. These velvet frames can be made either by mitring the corners or by sewing the canvas directly on to a flat piece. The trouble with the latter method is that you get a lump where the canvas is folded under. You can overcome this problem with embroidery, as shown here, but only if your canvas is reasonably straight. Distorted work will pull the velvet and spoil your cushion, so mitring is recommended for distorted canvases.

To make the cushion as shown, trim the canvas, leaving just two holes of mesh along each side. Lay the work flat on the velvet and baste it in place. Using a large sewing needle with a sharp point, sew a line of chain stitch in wool all the way around, covering the raw canvas as you go. Be careful not to pull the yarn too tight or the fabric will pucker.

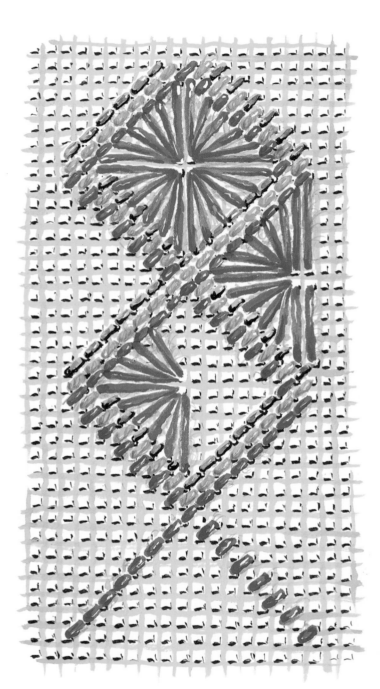

Border stitch pattern

LITTLE PINK FLOWER

FINISHED STITCHED AREA
$10\frac{1}{4} \times 8\frac{3}{4}$in (26 × 22cm), excluding the chain stitched edge

STITCHES
Tent stitch (basketweave) or half cross stitch, french knots, and surface embroidery in long stitch (optional)

MATERIALS
15 × 13in (38 × 33cm) of interlock canvas, 12 holes per inch (2.5cm)
Size 20 tapestry needle

ROWAN NEEDLEPOINT WOOL

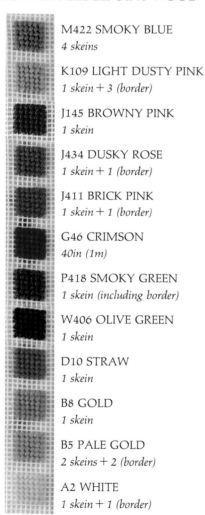

M422 SMOKY BLUE
4 skeins

K109 LIGHT DUSTY PINK
1 skein + 3 (border)

J145 BROWNY PINK
1 skein

J434 DUSKY ROSE
1 skein + 1 (border)

J411 BRICK PINK
1 skein + 1 (border)

G46 CRIMSON
40in (1m)

P418 SMOKY GREEN
1 skein (including border)

W406 OLIVE GREEN
1 skein

D10 STRAW
1 skein

B8 GOLD
1 skein

B5 PALE GOLD
2 skeins + 2 (border)

A2 WHITE
1 skein + 1 (border)

ANNA MARIA CUSHION

I named this after Anna Maria Garthwaite, as her work has given me so much pleasure. There is a wonderful book of the V&A collections entitled *Silk Designs of the Eighteenth Century* by Natalie Rothstein. It contains over 370 colour plates, many of which illustrate designs by Anna Maria and by James Leman, and they are magnificent. My eyes translate them into needlepoint patterns every time I open the book.

This silk design, with its flying petals and whimsical stalks, was very appealing, and though thin lines can be difficult to achieve in needlepoint, I thought they might work against a light background. Using Anna Maria's exotic flower shapes, the design for this cushion was quite simple to put together. I traced the flowers and bunched them together to fit the cushion shape. I used watercolour pencils to colour the design before starting my stitching, but changes were made, for what works on paper does not always translate successfully. The wool colours come out much darker than they look in the hand.

When choosing the colours, I started with the blues and rusts and greens of the original, then added shades that were quite close to these base colours, thereby accentuating them rather than changing them. The pale yellow background was the best colour that I could find to set off both the spring and autumn tints that make up this design. The pale orange stripe around the edge was put in to match a piece of material that I had fancied for piping. It is a good idea to look around at your furnishings and spot colour details that you like so that you can pick them up in your needlepoint by including a few french knots or motifs in backgrounds.

Facing page: The relatively simple flower forms in this silk weaving design by Anna Maria Garthwaite (dated 1742) have been bunched together to create the Anna Maria Cushion (overleaf).

Following page: The Anna Maria Cushion is based on her silk design. The tartan frill and pale orange piping create a pretty frame for the flowers.

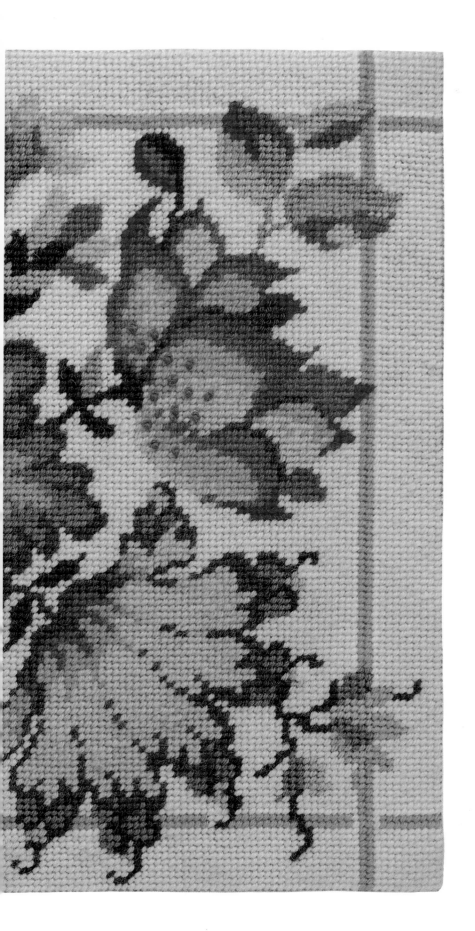

ANNA MARIA CUSHION

FINISHED STITCHED AREA
$14\frac{1}{4} \times 10\frac{1}{2}$in (36 × 27cm)
STITCH
Tent stitch (basketweave) or half cross stitch
MATERIALS
$20 \times 16\frac{1}{2}$in (50 × 42cm) or interlock canvas,
12 holes per inch (2.5cm)
Size 20 tapestry needle

ROWAN NEEDLEPOINT WOOL

V30 PALE LEMON
14 skeins

J83 PALE PINK
1 skein

E401 PALE APRICOT
1 skein

E20 PEACH
2 skeins

J412 DUSKY PINK
1 skein

G46 CRIMSON
1 skein

E147 TOFFEE
1 skein

P416 PALE MINT
2 skeins

P89 PALE JADE
1 skein

V135 GREEN
1 skein

R430 DARK GREEN
2 skeins

M88 SMOKY BLUE
2 skeins

M414 SEA BLUE
2 skeins

N48 LIGHT BLUE
1 skein

A110 BRIGHT WHITE
2 skeins

PRINCE ALBERT

The technique of outlining the pattern in a single colour is an easy solution for those of us who find drawing and painting difficult. It has the further advantage of reducing the amount of counting needed when you are copying. Once the outlines are there, you can fill in the colours with relative ease. I used this technique with my first pieces; looking back, they work well, and I have got over the feeling that I was cheating. Needlepoint techniques are different to those of painting, where you can shade and shape with relative ease.

Elongated diamonds are evocative of Victorian decoration, and stripes with patterns in them were also a recurring feature as I turned the pages

Above and right: Three albums of textile designs from Mulhouse were recently acquired by the V&A. The tiny posy, taken from one of the designs, was enlarged as the basis for the Prince Albert Cushion (page 6) and Chair Seat (right). Also used were other stylistic elements that feature strongly in the Mulhouse designs, including patterns in stripes, and motifs enclosed in squares, ovals or diamonds.

Prince Albert is probably the most Victorian pattern in this collection, with its deep but bright colours, blue background, black edgings and patterned striped border, but it is derived from a much earlier fabric design, dated 1790.

In 1986 the V&A purchased three albums of designs for printed textiles which originated in Mulhouse, a town on the French border with Germany. The designs range in date from about 1775 to the middle of the nineteenth century. Floral stylization is a major theme in these albums, and I chose a spray of flowers and leaves as the basis of the design, which I stitched in outline in black. Originally, I had not intended to do this, but when I drew the flower outlines with black felt-tip pen so that I could trace them on the canvas, I liked the Victorian effect.

of these albums. I wanted a striped background so that the pattern could easily be extended to cover furniture, without upsetting the scale of the design. An over-extended plain background can spoil the balance of a piece, causing pretty designs to look lost in the middle of a large chair seat or cushion. Most of the patterned stripes in these Mulhouse collections were too complicated to copy, so I made my own, taking the diamond shape of the centre and stitching little black diamonds into the ribbon stripes.

Having created a pattern that could be extended, I tried it out in practice by making it into a cover for a chair seat. I found a battered

Victorian dining chair in my local junk shop and had it restored. The chair had a front and back panel which also required needlepoint for upholstery. The obvious answer for the front was to repeat the flowers, but with a simpler design on the chair seat itself I might have echoed the pattern on the wood carving for the front panel.

The upholsterer told me that it was traditional to use a tartan pattern for the back. I thought this would be easy, so using the same colours I set to work. The next time I attempt a tartan I shall copy someone else's. Tartans are woven, but in needlepoint you have to pretend that the colours pass under each other and emerge in different places. I made so many mistakes and got so confused by this that I had to give it to someone else to finish, so I advise you to draw out a tartan with great care before attempting to stitch.

The choice of colours for Albert was really dictated by the colour impression of the Mulhouse books. Black backgrounds abound, bringing into sharp contrast the yellows, greens and pinky reds of the flowers, beloved of the Victorians. Those faded furnishing fabrics that we find in antique shops give a false impression of the bright furnishing colours that were actually used. I wonder why we have become so afraid of using colours today, but for those of you who prefer softer shades, this pattern would look lovely stitched in chalky pale pastels with pale grey outlines.

The Albert design can be applied to many different pieces of furniture, and would look good as a cushion, a stool top, a chair seat, or a bolster. The bolster would be stitched to the same dimensions as that on page 70, and made up in the same way. Alternatively, the design could be used as a stool top, as shown for the Malakoff Castle (see page 36). To make the Albert design into a stool top, extend the stripes to fit your piece of furniture. It would be advisable to consult with the upholsterer to see what margins he would need to work with, depending on the style of stool, the depth of the pad and other considerations.

To make it into a chair seat cover, refer to the guidelines at the end of this book. The two panels for the front and back of this chair would make pretty cushions and would be fun to put back to back, trimmed with black satin cord, as a double-sided needlepoint cushion.

The front panel of the Albert Chair (see also page 87) was designed to fit the back rest. It uses the same flower and leaf shapes as the chair seat. Trace the shapes, cut them out and re-group them until they fit the shape of your chair.

PRINCE ALBERT CHAIR SEAT AND CUSHION

This can be used either for a cushion or a chair seat. The finished stitched area of the chair seat shown here measured 19 × 15in (48 × 38cm), but these measurements can be adjusted by adding or subtracting background to fit your own chair (see also page 135). The wool quantities refer to the cushion.

STITCH
Tent stitch (basketweave) or half cross stitch

MATERIALS
De luxe mono canvas, 12 holes per inch (2.5cm), some 3in (7.5cm) larger all around than the finished embroidery
Size 20 tapestry needle

ROWAN NEEDLEPOINT WOOL

A62 BLACK
10 skeins

M111 BLUE
12 skeins

V617 PALE OLIVE GREEN
2 skeins

V105 OLIVE GREEN
6 skeins

T74 GRASS GREEN
1 skein

R73 DARK GREEN
2 skeins

P91 FIR TREE GREEN
10 skeins

J427 PINKY BROWN
2 skeins

H70 DARK PINK
9 skeins

G46 CRIMSON
1 skein

J424 SALMON PINK
1 skein

E20 PEACH
1 skein

E402 APRICOT
2 skeins

B6 YELLOW
7 skeins

A110 BRIGHT WHITE
1 strand

Following page: This chair needed another piece of upholstery for the back. I was told that a tartan or check pattern was traditional for this purpose, so created a pattern using the same palette though leaving out the dark greens.

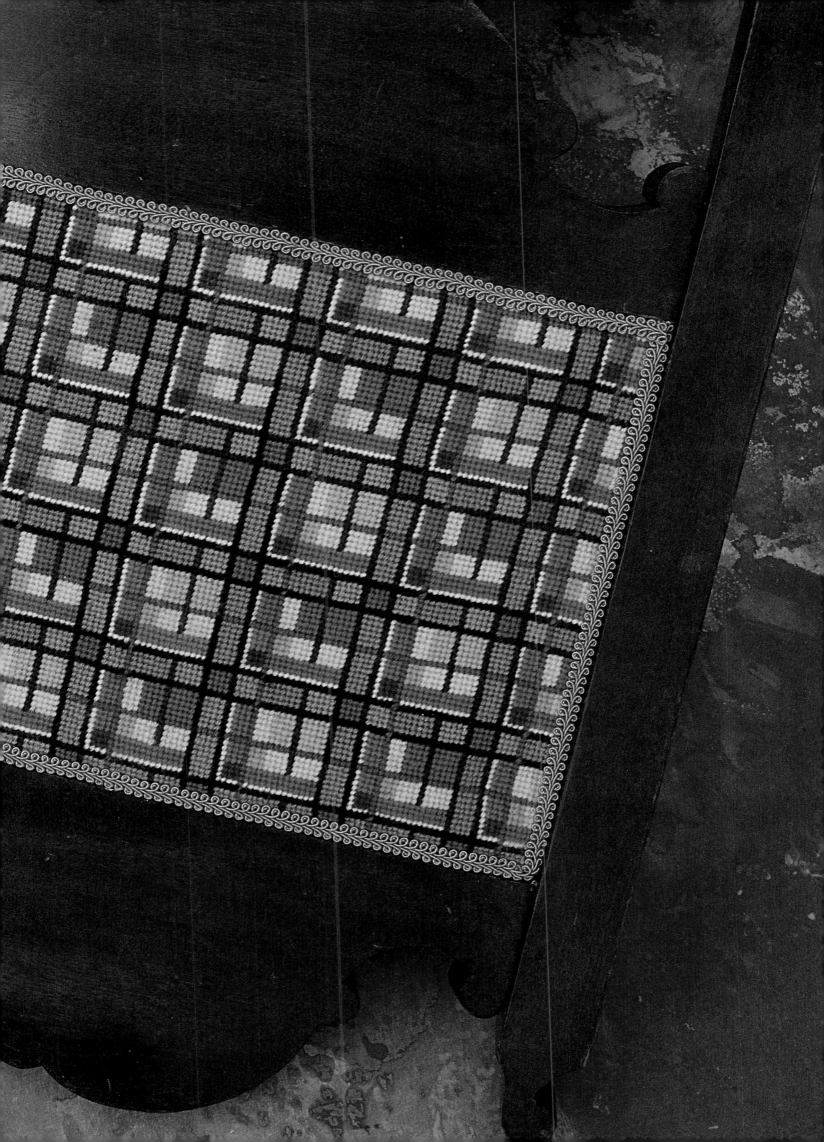

ALBERT CHAIR FRONT PANEL

TOP

FINISHED STITCHED AREA
$13\frac{1}{2} \times 8\frac{3}{4}$in (34 × 22cm)

STITCH
Tent stitch (basketweave) or half cross stitch

MATERIALS
20 × 15in (50 × 38cm) of interlock canvas, 12 holes per inch (2.5cm)
Size 20 tapestry needle

ROWAN NEEDLEPOINT WOOL

A62 BLACK
4 skeins

M111 BLUE
5 skeins

V105 OLIVE
2 skeins

V617 PALE OLIVE
2 skeins

T74 GRASS GREEN
1 skein

R73 DARK GREEN
1 skein

P91 FIR TREE GREEN
1 skein

J427 PINKY BROWN
2 skeins

H70 DARK PINK
1 skein

G46 CRIMSON
1 skein

J424 SALMON PINK
1 skein

E20 PEACH
1 skein

E402 APRICOT
1 skein

B6 YELLOW
1 skein

A110 BRIGHT WHITE
1 strand

ALBERT CHAIR BACK PANEL

Draw your tartan on graph
paper. For quantities, you
will need 36in (1m) of wool
for every 100 stitches.

STITCH
Tent stitch (basketweave) or half
cross stitch

MATERIALS
Interlock canvas, 12 holes
per inch (2.5cm)
Size 20 tapestry needle

ROWAN NEEDLEPOINT WOOL

A62 BLACK

M111 BLUE

T74 GRASS GREEN

V105 OLIVE

V617 PALE OLIVE

V664 STRAW GREEN

J427 PINKY BROWN

H70 DARK PINK

J424 SALMON PINK

E20 PEACH

E402 APRICOT

B6 YELLOW

A110 BRIGHT WHITE

DRIED FLOWER BASKET

Facing page: Dried Flower Basket is most enjoyable to stitch. The single small flowers give the impression of a lot of detail without being hard on the eyes. French knots have been used in abundance, and the long stitch used for the basket adds textural interest.

The unlikely origin of this design is a collection of bookbinders' endpapers. The V&A have boxes of papers from all periods, illustrating a huge variety of techniques, ranging from marbling and batique to embossing and lithography. Marbled papers were first imported into England in the middle of the seventeenth century, as wrappers for toys from Nuremberg. The wrappers were sold to bookbinders who used them as end and lining papers.

Many of the papers had most unusual repeating motifs that looked to me like the extraordinary flowerheads that dried flower specialists produce nowadays, often in deep bright colours that are a far cry from the faded dusty blooms that were the dried flowers of the past. I particularly liked the pattern that resembled jolly smiling faces with punk hairdos (see overleaf). The basket paper clinched the idea for this design. I wanted to include a marbled paper, but found it difficult to reproduce in stitching — though I have seen it done well since completing this design. The nearest I got to marbling was with the tablecloth, which reflects the shapes and colours of a paper that had particular appeal. The endpaper pattern samples shown overleaf are just a few that gave me the flower heads for this Dried Flower Basket.

The basket itself is stitched with two shades of embroidery cotton, threaded together on the

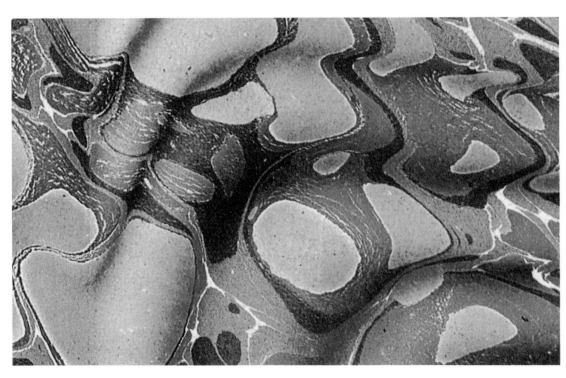

A marbled endpaper pattern from the extensive collection at the V&A. The colours were used for the tablecloth in the picture (right).

To embroider the basket, work the plain blue stitches first.

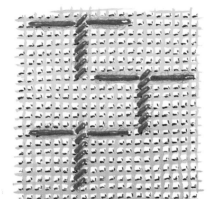

Then thread the two embroidery threads onto the needle together and make the long stitches.

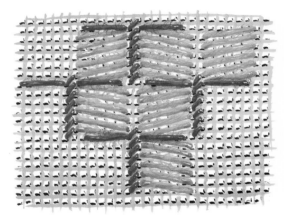

Finish with the tent stitches, again using these double threads.

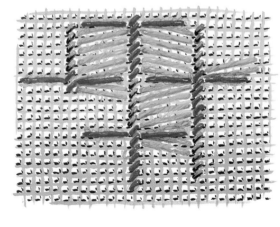

needle and allowed to mix at random. Looking at baskets, you will see that the light catches each strand of cane, creating a strong contrast of light and shade.

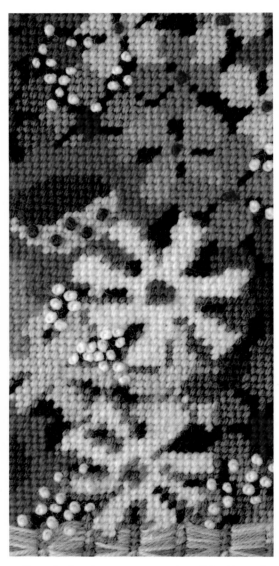

French knots appear again, this time in abundance, softening the edges in the way that gypsophila does to a bunch of flowers. You can add as many or as few as you like. If you are unhappy about a shape, a french knot can often mask it well. See page 133 for detailed instructions.

Incidentally, my family think a plain background would improve this design.

DRIED FLOWER BASKET

To make this into a picture, the top was curved – a picture framer will do this for you – but for a cushion it is squared off.

FINISHED STITCHED AREA
18 × 16in (46 × 41cm)

STITCH
Tent stitch (basketweave) or half cross stitch, long stitch, and french knots

MATERIALS
24 × 22in (60 × 55in) of interlock canvas,
12 holes per inch (2.5cm)
Size 20 tapestry needle
32yds (29m) each of stranded embroidery cotton in straw and pale grey, for the basket

ROWAN NEEDLEPOINT WOOL

A625 CHARCOAL
2 skeins

M53 PRUSSIAN BLUE
3 skeins

M414 MID-BLUE
9 skeins

P100 JADE
2 skeins

P421 GREY GREEN
2 skeins

V617 PALE OLIVE
3 skeins

B152 MUSTARD
2 skeins

E104 AMBER
3 skeins

E402 APRICOT
2 skeins

A2 WHITE
4 skeins

L120 PALE MAUVE
14 skeins

J410 ROSE PINK
3 skeins

J411 DUSKY PINK
3 skeins

L423 PURPLE
2 skeins

H85 MAROON
2 skeins

B6 YELLOW
4 skeins

Mixed embroidery cotton
STRAW AND PALE GREY

Japanese Stencil Designs

The V&A collection of several thousand Japanese stencils was acquired during the 1880s and 1890s. Many of the motifs reach far back into the history of Japanese design and have become

This Japanese stencil design inspired Haiku Birds (opposite). The main motifs have been taken, but simplified slightly, and the birds are from another stencil pattern (overleaf).

Facing page: Haiku Birds is shown here without the border (see overleaf for Greek key style bordered cushion). Simple patterns, such as this one which is repeated around a square, are relatively easy to execute, and work well on cushions.

traditional to the medium. The fish, birds and bamboo subjects are familiar from the cotton kimono-style dressing gowns that the Japanese export all over the world and from the beautiful papers and cards that are readily available in the

West. However, the organic patterns that looked like specimens seen through a microscope were unexpected, and the Greek-key borders to many of the stencils were a surprise. Haiku Birds has a border of this type, which you can either use as a box edge or leave flat for a big cushion.

The simple but effective blue and white of traditional Japanese stencil patterns, originally used for fabrics, never date. A little book of selected Japanese stencil patterns from the V&A archives enabled me to study and trace the designs, to enlarge the patterns and mix them up. Normally, the stencil shapes were used by Japanese textile designers to make white patterns on indigo-dyed fabric, so the V&A book, in which the stencils are given in blue, effectively shows negative images. With all this in mind, Haiku Birds is probably a very western interpretation of Japanese motifs.

The fine lines and tiny patterns that abound in the V&A collections are impossible to reproduce in needlepoint on a relatively large gauge canvas, but the stencil effect — where the patterns are broken by 'bridges' that hold the stencil together — are effective and simple to re-create. The freshness of the blue and white is a relief after the heavy Victorian colours with complicated shading that are so often associated with needlepoint, but I did find it necessary to use at least four shades of blue to make it come alive. Single colours in needlepoint need other shades to set them off.

Detail of a Japanese Stencil design — the simple clearly defined shapes require no complicated shading.

Facing page: Haiku Birds has here been given a border pattern. It can be made into either a simple or box-edged cushion. The cord trim is handmade, using needlepoint wool.

Haiku Birds is like a stencil used four times around a square. If you are designing a pattern along these lines, the simplest way is to photocopy it so that you have got four pieces exactly the same. Cut them out and position them on a sheet of paper the size of the finished cushion. When they are all in place, trace the first pattern onto the canvas and make some marks where the other three should start. When you have stitched the first pattern, make a chart of the stitches and colours on graph paper to copy for the rest. As you turn the corner you will find the stitches will be going in a different direction in relation to the pattern, so this graph is invaluable as a working guide. You may have to make some slight adjustments to stop parts of the pattern from joining up or becoming gappy, which tends to happen when a turn causes the stitches to lie in a different direction from the master pattern. This explanation may seem complicated, but I think you will understand the moment you start to undertake the work.

THE BOX-EDGED CUSHION

To stitch the box-edged cushion, it is
necessary to create a clean fold line between
the border and the cushion top. This is
achieved by stitching the top and edge
separately, leaving a thread of unstitched
canvas between the two. Do not carry threads
under this line. There should be three lines of
white stitching above the border pattern, then
one thread of unstitched canvas, and then the
white background of the cushion top. The box
edge should be 20 stitches deep.

MATERIALS
17 × 14in (43 × 35cm) of furnishing fabric
12in (30cm) zip to match
1½yd (1.4m) of braid trim
13in (33cm) square cushion pad
Matching thread

Cut the fabric widthwise in two and insert the
zip (see page 134). Trim spare canvas from the
completed needlepoint, leaving a margin of
about 1in (2.5cm). Snip away the canvas in the
corners, as shown, leaving a margin of a scant
½in (12mm). Fold down the box edge along the
line of unstitched canvas and oversew the
corners to create the box shape.

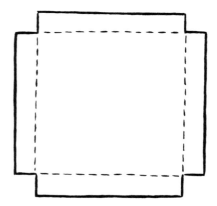

Turn this inside out and, with the zip
partially open and with right sides together,
machine your furnishing fabric to the box. It is
easier to stitch each side individually rather
than attempting to stitch around sharp corners.
Turn the cushion right side out and insert the
cushion pad. To finish, stitch braid trim to
cover the line of raw canvas.

HAIKU BIRDS

FINISHED STITCHED AREA

The box-edged cushion measures $13\frac{1}{4} \times 12\frac{3}{4}$in ($34 \times 32.5$cm), with an edge $1\frac{3}{4}$in (4.5cm) deep. The cushion cannot be an exact square, because the canvas holes are not perfect squares. The flat version, with a key border, measures $17 \times 16\frac{1}{2}$in (43×42cm). Both are stitched from the same pattern.

STITCH

Tent stitch (basketweave) or half cross stitch

MATERIALS

For either cushion — 23in (58cm) square of interlock canvas, 12 holes per inch (2.5cm) Size 20 tapestry needle

ROWAN NEEDLEPOINT WOOL

A110 BRIGHT WHITE
30 skeins

M88 SLATE BLUE
3 skeins

M111 DUSKY BLUE
5 skeins

N50 MID-BLUE
4 skeins

M49 SEA BLUE
4 skeins

JAPANESE PETALS

Japanese Petals also originates from the little book of stencils already mentioned. I took the petal shapes directly from a small pattern and floated them over a stylized version of swirling motifs that appear in many different guises in Japanese art.

This piece is slightly more geometric than most of my designs, but I was looking for something a little different that a man might like to stitch. Many men dislike stitching flowers, but they often enjoy repeating geometric designs that require accuracy. I have chosen a different selection of blues to that used for Haiku Birds, but if you want to make it match the latter, use the Haiku shades instead; they will work just as well.

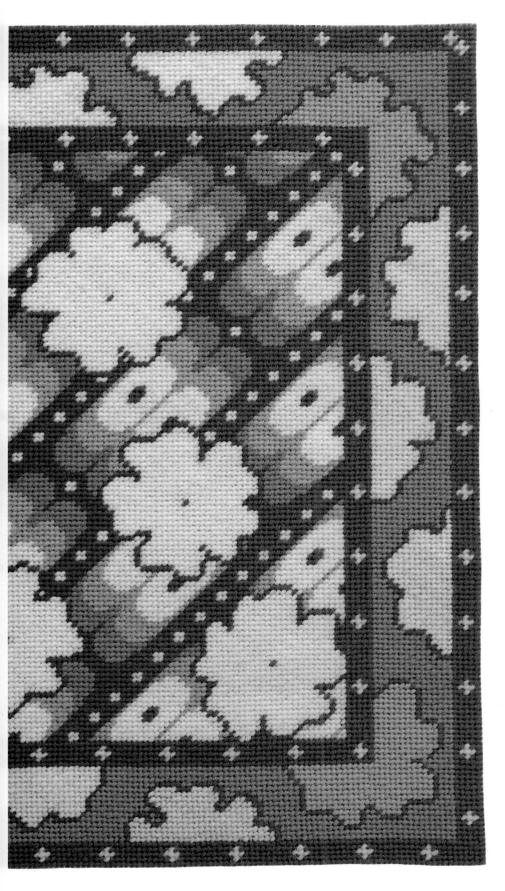

JAPANESE PETALS

FINISHED STITCHED AREA
13¾in (35cm) square

STITCH
Tent stitch (basketweave) or half cross stitch

MATERIALS
20in (50cm) square of interlock canvas, 12
holes per inch (2.5cm)
Size 20 tapestry needle

ROWAN NEEDLEPOINT WOOL

A110 BRIGHT WHITE
12 skeins

N48 PALE SKY BLUE
8 skeins

N50 MID-BLUE
8 skeins

N141 BRIGHT BLUE
13 skeins

*Facing page:
Floating Petals is
derived from a
Japanese stencil
design, but treated
in a different way
to Haiku Birds.
One simple pattern
of uncluttered petal
outlines is floated at
random across a
complicated
geometric
background.*

THE WALLPAPER COLLECTION

The V&A archives house some wonderful examples of wallpapers, including both hand-produced and machine-printed designs. A border paper was the inspiration for Double Damask, and I had little to do to transpose it into a needlepoint design. I changed the colours simply because so many people like pinks and reds, but it would work equally well with the blues and greys of the original.

Wallpapers provide an excellent design source. Conceived for domestic use, the scale and colours are often perfect for needlepoint. The same limitations face both the wallpaper designer and the stitcher. Colours come in solid blocks rather than subtle watery shading, and relatively few colours are used because the more you use the more expensive it is to produce the wallpaper. The same restriction applies to printed canvases, so there is always the search for a balance. I usually allow myself 15 colours when designing for printed canvas, but am thrilled when I find I have used less without any detriment to the finished design. The colours themselves appear to change when combined with different shades. A dusky purple next to green can look brown, but next to a deep pink it looks much bluer. Once you discover this you can incorporate a lot of apparent colour variations without using more shades. Wallpaper designers are masters of this art.

Backgrounds are often neglected in traditional designs, which I think can be a missed oppor-

tunity. Having stitched the interesting parts, many people give up when faced with acres of beige to fill in. I think of backgrounds as wallpapers, so it is back to the archives for inspiration. Dots, stripes or tiny shapes can be so simple but very effective and make interesting

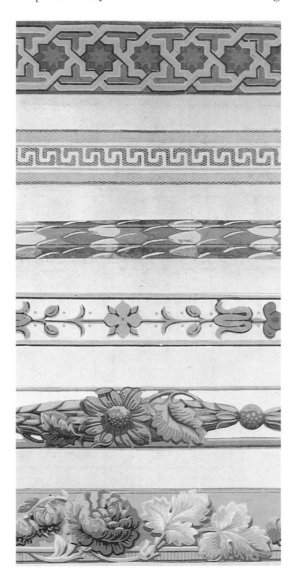

Some wallpaper border patterns from the V&A collections — Double Damask is based on the design at the bottom. The third one down would make a lovely needlepoint border.

Facing page: Double Damask is shown as a cushion and as a stool top. The cord trim on the cushion is handmade using needlepoint wool. Wallpaper patterns often translate well into needlepoint.

stitching. The idea for the background for Double Damask came from the effect of damask weave on table cloths. I inherited an enormously long one and was told that that size was called a 'double damask'. The name fitted my design to perfection.

Double Damask can be used as a large cushion or stool top, as shown here, but also as a bolster if the size is slightly enlarged to measure $18 \times 22\frac{1}{2}$in (47×57cm), see page 70.

Damask Rose is a natural progression from Double Damask. It is exciting to make that big bloom even bigger by using large gauge canvas. The rose is an exact copy of that in Double Damask, but I changed the leaves. I had just finished stitching a few small leaves for the Fantasia chair and had that same urge to stitch them on a bigger scale. The technique of using dots of colour works well on large mesh – Kaffe Fassett does this wonderfully – so I tried it as a contrast to the very defined shapes of the rose petals. I then put dots into the background as well, to emphasize the pointilliste effect.

Once again, it was looking closely at wallpapers that gave me the courage to mix rust, blue, yellow and purple into my foliage, as well as the more usual greens and browns. The colour limitations for producing wallpapers force designers to be endlessly resourceful, so they often use flower colours to create leaves as well. Stitchers are faced with fewer limitations, but from examining wallpapers I have learned that leaves can be more exciting if unexpected shades are added and can also be used as vehicles for colours that I want to include somewhere, but not as a major element in the design. I would encourage people to try changing a colour in the leaves if they want to fit this design into their own colour scheme.

Facing page: The bloom from Double Damask (see previous page) has been transferred to a large gauge canvas, and set among more modern foliage to create the dramatic effect of Damask Rose. Changing the scale of a design can alter its character quite unexpectedly.

DOUBLE DAMASK

FINISHED STITCHED AREA
$20\frac{1}{2} \times 15\frac{3}{4}$in ($52 \times 40$cm)

STITCH
Tent stitch (basketweave) or half cross stitch, and french knots to finish the flower centres

MATERIALS
26×22in (66×56cm) of interlock canvas, 12 holes per inch (2.5cm)
Size 20 tapestry needle

ROWAN NEEDLEPOINT WOOL

P655 DARK PINE
4 skeins

P91 FIR TREE GREEN
3 skeins

P418 SMOKY GREEN
3 skeins

P417 MID-GREEN
3 skeins

V106 OLIVE
2 skeins

V31 PALE LEMON
1 skein

D72 OCHRE
1 skein

K95 PURPLY PINK
2 skeins

K96 MAGENTA
2 skeins

G435 CRIMSON
1 skein

J68 PINK
2 skeins

L423 PURPLE
3 skeins

M422 SKY GREY
16 skeins

Z64 PALE GREY
13 skeins

DAMASK ROSE

FINISHED STITCHED AREA
$17\frac{3}{4} \times 16\frac{1}{2}$in (45 × 42cm)

STITCH
Tent stitch (basketweave) – half cross stitch
would give too thin a finish; use two threads
in the needle throughout.

MATERIALS
24 × 22in (60 × 56cm) of interlock canvas,
7 holes per inch (2.5cm)
Size 20 tapestry needle

ROWAN NEEDLEPOINT WOOL

P655 DARK PINE
2 skeins

P91 FIR TREE GREEN
3 skeins

P418 SMOKY GREEN
4 skeins

P417 MID-GREEN
5 skeins

V31 PALE LEMON
2 skeins

A2 WHITE
4 skeins

J68 PALE PINK
2 skeins

K95 PURPLY PINK
2 skeins

K96 MAGENTA
2 skeins

G46 CRIMSON
2 skeins

L423 PURPLE
3 skeins

M52 PRUSSIAN BLUE
3 skeins

Z64 GREY
16 skeins

D9 OLD GOLD
2 skeins

QUEEN VICTORIA

The V&A houses a collection of nearly 800 patterns for printed cottons, the years between 1790 and 1810 being particularly well represented. This is often referred to as the golden age of printed textiles, and leafing through the volumes one can see why. Most are breathtakingly pretty; many are extremely inventive, and the use of colour is stunning. The border patterns were reproduced by means of wooden printing blocks and were used for handkerchiefs, tablecloths and shawls, as well as for furnishing fabrics.

They seemed an obvious choice on first acquaintance, but when I started to look more closely I found the detail too fine and the patterns too intricate for needlepoint. I had to simplify drastically to make them work. For the centre panel of the cushion, I took a border pattern with relatively simple flowers and interesting leaf configurations. Using white and very pale yellow, pink and mauve, I managed to get something of the flower shapes, but lost the impression of petal on petal. The leaves were much easier, but need more colour variation than

the original. The border is a tiny scalloped edge pattern blown up to about twenty times its original size.

As this is quite a heavy pattern, something was needed between the border and the central piece to frame the rather delicate flowers, almost like a mount for a picture. I liked the effect produced by the dashes of deep pink on the buds, and felt that this could be taken further. I used long stitch simply because it offered a speedy way of seeing if twisting stripes would work, but left them in as the effect of a change in stitch pattern helped to create the break I was seeking. Long stitch can offer a useful way of trying out colours before committing yourself to hours of work. It is also quick to unpick.

When putting a border onto a cushion, it is as well to remember that once the pad is in, the shape will change and a lot of the edge will be lost in the resulting curve. It is therefore best to concentrate the pattern on the centre and choose a border that is simple but strong. It may look overwhelming when laid flat, but provides a frame when padded and on your sofa.

Facing page: Queen Victoria was based on the shapes and leaf configurations of this textile pattern from the Mulhouse albums. The challenge was to convert the delicacy of the original into needlepoint.

Following page: The heavy border of the Queen Victoria design is softened by the cushion padding. The matching cord is handmade from needlepoint wool.

These dear little shapes come from an edging pattern to a textile border design. They have been enlarged to make a big border for Queen Victoria (overleaf and page 3).

QUEEN VICTORIA

FINISHED STITCHED AREA
14½ × 13½in (37 × 34cm)

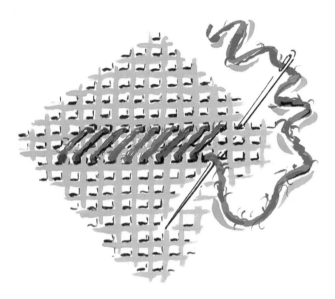

STITCH
Tent stitch (basketweave) or half cross stitch,
long diagonal stitch and cross stitch (optional)

MATERIALS
20in (50cm) square of interlock canvas, 12
holes per inch (2.5cm)
Size 20 tapestry needle

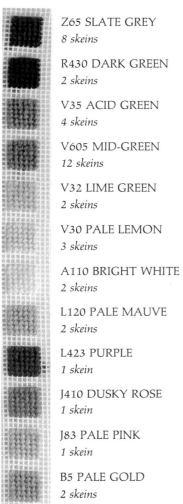

ROWAN NEEDLEPOINT WOOL

Z65 SLATE GREY
8 skeins

R430 DARK GREEN
2 skeins

V35 ACID GREEN
4 skeins

V605 MID-GREEN
12 skeins

V32 LIME GREEN
2 skeins

V30 PALE LEMON
3 skeins

A110 BRIGHT WHITE
2 skeins

L120 PALE MAUVE
2 skeins

L423 PURPLE
1 skein

J410 DUSKY ROSE
1 skein

J83 PALE PINK
1 skein

B5 PALE GOLD
2 skeins

HELPFUL INFORMATION

I am often asked what the difference is between needlepoint and tapestry. The word 'tapestry' is often used to describe this craft, but technically tapestry is a type of weaving; some argue that needlepoint is also incorrect in this context, as it could cause confusion with needlepoint lace. Canvaswork is the correct word. However, as this is not in common usage, it conjures up rug-making to many, and nothing at all to the majority. Needlepoint is the term we have chosen to use as it is understood and commonly used throughout the English-speaking world, whatever linguistic purists may suggest!

Most of the pieces in this book have been embroidered in tent stitch (see page 132), though I have scattered french knots, which I love, over some designs, and have used a variety of stitches in a few projects that are intended for the more adventurous to try. Rather than repeating the basic instructions for each piece, I have given some general instructions and guidelines below, and I urge even the experienced to glance through them.

NEEDLEPOINT CANVAS

Throughout this book I have used Zweigart interlock canvas, in which the threads are locked together, giving a little more resistance to distortion than mono (single thread) canvas. My favourite canvas is de luxe mono, the threads of which have been polished before weaving. The yarn runs through the canvas beautifully, but there are problems. It is not only extremely expensive, but it can distort badly and presents difficulties to printers.

If you are an experienced stitcher, with good tension, working on unprinted canvas and using a frame, then de luxe mono is the best. However, the interlock is a close second. Double thread (Penelope) canvas is much softer and is therefore prone to distortion. It is designed to allow tiny stitches to be inserted between the threads for details such as faces.

Most of the pieces illustrated are worked on canvas with 12 holes per inch (2.5cm) as it allows detail without straining the eyes too much. You can change the size of the finished piece by changing the gauge of the canvas. The Rowan needlepoint wool covers canvas with 12 or 14 holes per inch well. We do not recommended it for 10 holes unless you stitch quite loosely, and even then if you are putting in a dark background it is wise to paint the canvas with fabric paint first to prevent the white showing through.

This general advice about canvas assumes that you are using tent (basketweave) or half cross stitch. For fancy stitches, you must experiment a little, as each stitch gives different coverage. For very long stitches, you will need a smaller gauge canvas, but for patterns where

Facing page: Detail from Dried Flower Basket; a fringe or shade card (top right) is a useful tool when choosing colours for a design. Thread wool samples onto a card and write the shade numbers against them to avoid making mistakes when stitching in bad light.

several stitches are piled on top of one another (creating stars for instance) you will need a larger gauge or a finer thread.

Whichever canvas you choose to work with, remember to add at least 3in (7.5cm) as a margin around the piece of work you plan. Narrow margins can make the work difficult to hold when you are stitching at the edge, and impossible to work on a frame.

NEEDLES

'Tapestry' needles have a rounded end to push through the canvas and past previous stitches without breaking into them. The right size of needle is important if you are to feel comfortable with your work. A Size 20 needle fits a 12 or 14 gauge canvas, but you will need a larger one –

Size 18 – for 10 holes to the inch. On canvas with 7 holes to the inch, use a Size 16 with two strands of wool in the needle.

FRAMES

There is no doubt that the best finish is achieved by using a frame. There is something very ladylike about sitting down at your needlepoint frame with your wools in a basket at your feet. For most of us, however, that type of life is a fantasy. Frames are a matter of personal taste and I love to use one. Most of the time, unfortunately, I am stitching on the train, in an aeroplane or collapsed in front of the television at the end of a long day. A lot of the work for this book was stitched in bed in the early hours of the morning, when the light is good and there are no

It is an easy and quick job to pin the canvas to the frame. Simple stretcher frames are practical, portable, and easy to use (see page 141).

interruptions. Before going to sleep a small block of background was often achieved. A frame does not really fit into my hectic lifestyle.

If you are using a frame, use two hands. Put the needle down through the canvas with your left hand and pull it through underneath with your right hand. Do not yank the wool, but pull it through gently. Left-handed people should reverse the hands.

For diagonal tent (basketweave) stitch, which I always recommend, you will need a flat frame rather than a rolling one. If you roll up canvas that has been worked on one corner and not on the opposite one the canvas will be loose on one side, defeating the purpose of the frame. I like to see the whole piece of work in front of me and use simple stretcher frames, with the work pinned on with drawing pins (thumb tacks).

If you are not using a frame, either bind the edges of the canvas with masking tape or fold them over and machine stitch around. This prevents canvas threads from snagging on your clothes and scratching your skin. Roll the work up so that you can hold it in your left hand while stitching with your right. Try not to scrunch up the canvas, as this will encourage it to distort.

YARN

The yarn quantities recommended for the projects cannot be treated as absolutely accurate, as everyone uses different amounts. Yarn quantities present a big problem for kit producers. For these projects, we have assumed a length of 60in (1.5m) of yarn per square inch (2.5cm square) using tent (basketweave) stitch. Stitch a test square to see if this is more or less what you need. If you use half cross stitch, you will require around 30 per cent less wool than if you use basketweave.

WORKING FROM THE BOOK

Each needlepoint design is accompanied by illustrations of the original source material and a description of how this was used to create a piece of work. Colour selection and specific techniques are also discussed, but as the basic skills are the same for all the pieces they are discussed here. Following each introduction is a photograph of the worked canvas laid flat. These photographs are included to show how colours work together, how curves are achieved and how french knots and stitch variations look close up. The canvas gauge, needle size and the Rowan yarn shade numbers and quantities are alongside each photograph. Some people may find this sufficient to work from but, if not, charts are available by mail order (see page 141).

GETTING YOUR DESIGN ON CANVAS

Start by tracing or drawing the main outlines of the design on a piece of white paper. If it needs enlarging or reducing in size, take it to your local photocopying shop and give them the dimensions you are seeking. Draw around the outlines of your drawing or photocopy with a black felt-tip pen. Place your canvas on top of this and fix the two together with masking tape. If you find it difficult to see the lines, tape both to the window. Using a waterproof marker (I use a pale grey one), trace the outlines onto the canvas. You can now paint in the details, or just roughly mark the areas as you go along. Things inevitably change as you work, so do not put too much detail in to start with. Dark lines may show through if stitched over with a light-coloured wool, so take care. Put a large white table napkin on your lap when working, so that you can see the grey lines very clearly.

Following page: Crocodil is surrounded by some of the tools and materials used in the design process. Cutting out patterns and pasting them up, and then painting and colouring are the fun side of creating a design. Take lots of photocopies and try out different colour combinations.

ACHIEVING A GOOD FINISH

It appears to me that there are two basic rules for an even finish and a reasonably straight canvas:

- natural tension
- diagonal tent stitch

Tight tension is the biggest killer of needlepoint embroideries, and the importance of this simple fact cannot be over-emphasized. So often I see the canvases to which hours of loving care have been taken in stitching the pattern beautifully, only for the whole effect to be spoiled by stitching that is too tight. People are afraid that looser stitches will look uneven, but the opposite is true. The tension is created by two things – the pulling of the thread through the canvas, and the stitch that comes after the one that you have just done. This is simple to explain: it is sensible to bring your needle up in an empty square and down in a full one. When you push the needle down through the canvas in a square where there is already a stitch, your action tightens that stitch very slightly. If the stitch was not too tight to start with, a nice even finish is achieved.

When you start a stitch in a hole that already contains a stitch, you loosen that stitch, which can cause unevenness. Sometimes there is no choice except to come up in a hole where there is already a stitch. In this case, be sure that you stab the needle from underneath rather than completing the whole stitch (down and up) in one motion. If you are using a frame, you will be doing this anyway.

The second recommendation is that you master diagonal tent stitch (basketweave). This seems difficult to grasp at first, and many people don't even attempt to use it on details. I use it everywhere possible, including stripes that are only two stitches wide. It gives a much more even finish than any other tapestry-effect stitch;

handled properly, it will reduce distortion almost to nothing. In addition, it gives a more lasting wear than half cross stitch, which, if pulled tight, can result in gappy stitches and an almost transparent finish when held up to the light. I can tell at a glance where diagonal tent stitch has been used, and it always looks better. Vertical tent stitch, sometimes known as continental stitch, pulls the canvas into trapeziums with uncanny ease.

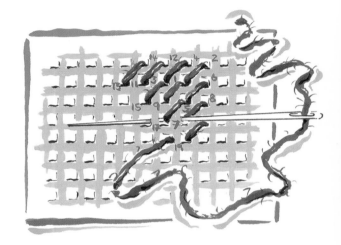

DIAGONAL TENT STITCH

The diagram shows how to use basketweave, starting at the top right-hand corner of a piece of work – the starting point for almost everything. The section to be filled could be background or it could be a leaf or petal. Whatever it is, the principles are the same: bring the needle up at 1 and down at 2, up at 3 and down at 4 and so on. The rows are worked diagonally across the canvas, up and down, working towards the top of the design on the up row and towards the right-hand side of the design on the down row. I think of each stitch as filling in a gap between the stitches of the previous row. It takes a little practice to get used to, but the results are well worth the effort.

To start, thread the needle and put a knot in the end of the yarn. Put the needle down through the canvas about ½in (12mm) away from the point where you want to make your first stitch. Pull it through to the back until the knot is all that is left on the front of the canvas. Start stitching towards the knot. When you reach it, cut it off. The loose thread underneath will have been stitched in by this time. To finish, run the thread under a few stitches at the back.

FRENCH KNOTS

Bring the needle up through the canvas where you want the finished knot to be. Point the needle away from you and wrap the thread around the needle. Holding the thread taut with your left hand, turn the needle back and put it through the canvas.

SOME USEFUL HINTS

To minimize distortion of the canvas and ensure good coverage

- use a frame, if you are happy with one
- allow the wool to relax as you stitch by using natural tension – tight stitches will distort the canvas and may not cover well
- use diagonal tent (basketweave) stitch
- snip off loose ends to prevent tangles, especially where dark and light shades are adjacent – small bits of fluff can get into the pale shades, spoiling the colour

STARTING AND FINISHING

Threads that are too long will wear thin as you pull them through, and may knot and snag as you work. About 30in (76cm) is the maximum length, and many people recommend 20in (50cm). Using a frame reduces wear on the yarn and lessens the likelihood of knots.

When you are filling large areas of background in diagonal tent stitch, you may end up with a bumpy surface if you run the wool through the back on the diagonal. In this case, it is best to run the wool under a few stitches in a horizontal line.

ORDER OF STITCHING

Stitch the detailed areas first, and the background last. For designs with borders, complete the central design first, then the border, and lastly the background. However, if the border is a geometric pattern, stitch this first to ensure that it fits correctly. With geometric designs, build up your pattern bit by bit. If you start in one place and jump to another you may have difficulty in fitting the pattern together.

When stitching kits, remember that no canvas printing can be 100 per cent accurate, as the canvas itself varies and is rarely straight. If your printed design is not quite straight, use your common sense and mark a straight line to follow around the edges.

LEFT-HANDED STITCHERS

Canvases are usually designed to be stitched with the stitches lying from top right to bottom left. This is awkward if you are left handed. With many designs, it does not matter if you work them with the stitches lying the other way. If you are worried about this, however, turn the work through 90 degrees, so that the top of the pattern is on your right and the bottom on your left as you face it, and work with the stitches running from the top left-hand corner to the bottom right. When you have finished, the stitches will be facing the correct way.

STRETCHING YOUR CANVAS

There are many different methods of stretching. I use the following, and find it nearly always works (with some tightly-stitched canvases, nothing will be completely successful).

You will need a board for pinning out, drawing pins (thumb tacks), and something with an exact rightangle – either a set square, a dressmakers' square, an old picture mount or an empty picture frame will serve so long as it can provide a true rightangle.

First steam the canvas thoroughly, either using a steam iron or holding it over boiling water (do not expose any flesh – use rubber gloves). While it is still warm and damp (but not wet) pin it on the board, pulling it straight with

the right side facing you. Be careful – wet wood can stain. Pin the centre of each side first, putting the pins in the margin, about 1in (2.5cm) from the stitched edge, and then pin out toward the corners. Use your square to ensure that you are pinning it straight. Hold it over the steam again when it is straight on your board, then leave for a few days. The purpose of the steam is to soften the canvas and melt the dressing on the canvas slightly (overwetting will flush it out). The dressing will then dry on the canvas in the correct position.

If your canvas is badly distorted, pin a piece of sheeting to the board to prevent staining and pin the canvas on with the wrong side facing you. Brush with wallpaper paste and rub it in gently with your fingers. Leave for a few days.

MAKING A BASIC CUSHION

You will need a piece of furnishing fabric a bit larger than your stitched work and a zip about 3in (7.5cm) smaller than the width of the stitched canvas. Trim your canvas, leaving a margin of about four holes of canvas all the way around. Cut your backing fabric 3in (7.5cm) wider than this and 5in (13cm) longer. Cut the fabric in two across the width, about 6in (15cm) from the top.

Put the two pieces of fabric right sides together, and lay the zip along the cut line in a central position. With taylors' chalk or pins, mark where the zip starts and finishes. Machine up to this mark at each end (approximately $1\frac{1}{2}$in/4cm in from each edge). Lay the fabric flat on the ironing board and press the fold where the zip is to be inserted. Baste and then machine the zip in place. Leaving the zip partly open, put backing fabric and canvas with right sides together. Baste and stitch the two pieces together, running them through the machine with the canvas uppermost.

The machine stitches should run in the middle of the holes of the last line of stitching – if you go slowly this should not be difficult. If you stitch further in you will not get a clean fold, and if you machine further out the raw canvas will show. Take care over this; it is worth the effort. Snip across the corners and turn the work right side out. Ease the corners out, using your tapestry needle – you can get them quite crisp if you work at it gently.

If you are piping your cushion, you should machine the piping to the canvas then sew the back on by hand. It is impossible to get a neat finish using a machine without losing a lot of your stitching, which would be a pity. Piping helps to correct distorted canvases, especially if you sew the back on straight (it seems awkward when you are doing it) rather than following the shape of your canvas. When you put the pad in it helps pull the work in the right direction.

USING NEEDLEPOINT IN YOUR HOME
It is not practical for manufacturers to make kits for mounting onto furniture (except perhaps chair seats) as the sizes vary so much. Most of the items of furniture shown here come from junk shops: the three chairs, the Nut Tree child's chair, the Fantasia fireside chair and the firescreen mount (formerly a mirror frame) were all bought with needlepoint in mind. Having them upholstered was surprisingly inexpensive compared with buying new furniture. The valuable part is the needlepoint, and the challenge is designing something to fit.

COVERING CHAIR SEATS
It is necessary to make a template so that you are stitching the correct size of canvas. A piece of paper or old cotton sheeting can be draped over the chair, pinned in place and then cut to fit. Cut out the corners and along the edges where the fabric meets the wood. The result should look roughly the shape of the diagram shown. Be generous – the upholsterer will cut the edges, believe it or not, and needs a good margin with which to work. Pulled too tight, the canvas will be under great strain when sat on and may split. Using your template, trace the shape on the canvas. Make some marks where the canvas folds down the chair, so that your design is sympathetic to the shape of the seat.

Tent or cross stitch are recommended for upholstery, as they are hardwearing. Half cross stitch is too thin to wear well. De luxe mono canvas has the highest tension resistance, and is the best for chair seats.

CLEANING
Needlepoint wool is surprisingly resistant to dirt, but once washed will be less so, which is another reason why you should not overwet your canvas when stretching. Washing will also take out of the canvas the dressing which is needed to help keep it straight, and there is a danger that the canvas will shrink and cause the work to pucker. A good spray with a proprietory dirt repellent will give added protection, and will save the day if anything is spilt on it. If a piece is really dirty, dry cleaning is the best solution, but use a quality service, not a slot machine. Dry cleaning spray can be used to remove dirty spots. Vacuum the powder out when it is dry, rather than brushing it, which will damage the wool.

Your needlepoint should last for your grandchildren to enjoy, and the many hours of pleasure that you have had in stitching it make it into something special and valuable to you. It is worth taking good care of it. Happy stitching!

CONVERSION TABLES

The 200 Rowan Needlepoint colours are different intentionally from those of other brands. Listed below are the colours quoted for the designs in this book, with the nearest equivalents from Anchor and Paterna (Paternayan). In some places an equivalent is not to be found but the colours selected should work together.

The skein length of all three brands quoted is approximately 11 yards (10 metres). Check the skein band for length if using another brand. You may have to adjust the quantities, especially for background colours.

Paterna (Paternayan) Persian yarn is a stranded wool. Use two strands on 12 holes per inch canvas, three on 10 holes per inch and five or six strands on 7 holes per inch canvas.

	ROWAN	ANCHOR	PATERNA		ROWAN	ANCHOR	PATERNA		ROWAN	ANCHOR	PATERNA		ROWAN	ANCHOR	PATERNA
A	2	8002	261	H	659	8514	D115	M	151	8694	571	S	433	8984	687
	110	8000	260		602	8354	920		414	8788	504	T	38	9102	631
	625	9768	221		85	8404	900		413	8818	505		74	9156	612
	62	9800	220		132	8242	D211		49	8626	563	V	605	9016	604
B	152	8016	727		70	8422	911		111	8630	560		75	9162	694
	8	8040	733	J	424	8398	954		54	8838	510		31	9192	763
	5	8054	735		411	8368	D275		53	8794	502		30	8014	764
	6	8038	704		434	8506	923		52	8790	503		32	9094	695
	4	9522	445		145	8508	D123		88	8738	512		135	9172	694
	84	9382	465		427	9678	D133		422	8734	513		105	9308	652
	116	8056	773		83	8342	935	N	55	8688	543		106	9200	651
	131	8112	763		410	8414	934		125	8808	583		35	9198	670
D	72	8100	724		68	8502	964		50	8628	544		617	9306	653
	9	8024	731		69	8418	913		141	8690	542		664	9304	644
	10	8046	752		148	8504	924		122	8776	554		619	9254	645
E	79	8296	491		412	8348	D234		123	8802	555	W	117	9648	421
	20	8304	845	K	96	8490	352		48	8684	505		98	9372	461
	103	9442	886		95	8488	353		47	8814	546		407	9332	640
	401	9502	493		128	8522	303		63	8774	545		406	9290	D511
	402	9524	804		92	8524	322	P	655	8884	531		139	9292	451
	104	9446	413		425	8522	323		91	8924	520		150	9330	442
	147	9448	D419		109	8542	325		100	8922	521	X	28	9644	422
F	45	8240	950		429	9672	314		90	8938	D502		107	9642	431
	78	9558	872	L	652	8552	310		89	8918	523		87	9492	433
	24	8310	862		423	8548	312		418	9078	603	Y	82	9656	463
G	43	8440	942		149	8592	311		421	8878	D546		614	9482	455
	42	8216	941		130	8526	301		417	9018	604		58	9052	204
	46	8442	902		137	8546	313		416	9072	D556		3	9632	475
	435	8458	903		121	8586	333		665	8874	534	Z	65	8720	210
					127	8590	332	R	606	9180	600		61	9068	D346
					501	8608	341		430	9176	691		60	9774	202
					120	8582	334		73	9006	610		64	9790	212

THE ROWAN STORY

We are proud to announce the publication of *V&A Needlepoint Collection*. The first **Rowan-Anaya Original** to focus on needlepoint, it combines outstanding design with the range and quality of Rowan Yarns.

Home for Rowan is an old stone mill in a narrow green valley in the shadow of the Pennines overlooking Holmfirth. The name of this Yorkshire-based yarn marketing and design company has become synonymous with the revolution that has swept the needlecraft and handknitting industry and changed its image and practice forever. Working with the cream of contemporary knitting designers, including Kaffe Fassett, Edina Ronay and Susan Duckworth, Rowan Yarns has taken what was once a hobby into the realms of high fashion. Rowan's design collections are now in fashion journals worldwide, while every glossy home supplement bears tasteful evidence of Rowan's artistic craftwork. Our yarns are marketed worldwide, from Japan and Australia, to Finland and Italy, and the sheer appeal of the variety and subtlety of colours and textures, combined with our willingness to experiment, ensure our continuing success.

Karen Elder, who runs the Rowan Stitching Company — a subsidiary of Rowan Yarns — shares with me and my colleagues an eye for innovative use of colour, texture and design. She is responsible for commissioning an exclusive collection of new designs every year from top textile designers such as Lillian Delevoryas, Carrie White, Jamie and Jessie Seaton. Most recently, Karen has collaborated with the Victoria & Albert Museum, producing reworkings of historical pieces and new designs directly inspired by the artefacts in the Museum. Rowan Stitching and Rowan Yarns work closely but separately, with the common aim of maintaining high standards of design and quality in textile-related products.

Rowan-Anaya Originals set new standards in quality from the very best contemporary knitwear and needlepoint designers. They are produced with the same care and attention that is given to all Rowan products — whether it be shade cards or needlepoint kits — and the same eye for form and colour that has become the Rowan hallmark.

Stephen Sheard.

KITS AND STOCKISTS

Charts for all the designs in this book can be purchased by mail order. Many are available as kits.
The Rowan Stitching Company also offers a wide range of products and services to needlepointers, from
printed kits, to canvases that are custom drawn to fit your own furniture; from needlepoint wool to
plain canvas and needles. The Rowan making-up service can fulfil most requests for stretching
canvases, cushion finishing and braid making. Stools are also available.
For full information about stockists and mail order services, please write to The Rowan Stitching Company,
The River House, Wargrave, Berkshire RG10 8HD. Tel 0734 401005.
For details of where our kits are available overseas, please contact our agents, as listed below.

Australia
Tapestry Craft
32 York Street
Sydney
NSW 2000
Tel: (02) 298588

United States and Canada
Westminster Trading Corporation
5 Northern Boulevard
Amherst
New Hampshire 03031
USA
Tel: (603) 886 5041

Belgium
Hedera
Diestsestraat 172
B – 3000 Leuven
Tel: (016) 23 21 89

Denmark
Designer Garn
Vesterbro 33A
DK 9000
Aalborg
Tel: (98) 134824

Finland
Helmi Vuorelma – OY
Vesijarvenkatu 13
SF – 15141 Lahti
Tel: (18) 826 831

France
Laurence Roque
Le Comptoir des Ouvrages
69 Rue St Martin
Paris 4
Tel: 4272 2212

Iceland
Storkurinn
Kjorgardi
Laugavegi 59
ICE – 101 Reykjavik
Tel: (01) 18258

Ireland
Needlecraft
27/28 Dawson Street
Dublin 2
Tel: (01) 772493

Mexico
Estambresy Tejidos Finos S.A.D.C.V.
A.V. Michoacan 30 – A
Local 3 Esq Av Mexico
Col Hipodromo Condesa 06170
Tel: (05) 264 84 74

Sweden
Wincent
Sveavagen 94
113 50 Stockholm
Tel: (08) 673 7060

INDEX

ACKNOWLEDGEMENTS

This book is dedicated to Joan Downes, who taught me needlepoint and has been a good friend.

My family have been endlessly patient and helpful, as they always are with my projects. My mother kept the business going in my absence; my sister gave lots of practical help as well as making me laugh through the tedious bits, and my brother made the big stools from a yew tree in his garden. My book-keeper, Susan Johnson, has taken on lots of extra work while I worked on the book.

The ladies who have stitched for me need a special thank you. Kathryn Whitefoot, whose standards are exemplary, has been a tower of strength, and her mother Mrs Annan forgot housework to help me meet the deadline. Averil Cooper translated the Frogge and Crocodil and the Coptic Bird from colour transparencies and did a marvellous job.

Caroline Hall spent many weeks working on Malakoff Castle and produced something very special. Mrs Francis has stitched through migranes for this book; Margaret Jones has tackled difficult projects from sketchy notes, and Mrs Gregory has not only stitched but has given moral support as well. Sheila Coulson came into the picture late, but stitched night and day to help me.

Stephen Sheard of Rowan Yarns gave me the encouragement and confidence to do this, and helped solve the problems and deal with the traumas en route. Jane Lock of the V&A was a pleasure to work with and it was a bonus getting to know Linda Burgess, whose photographs I have admired for a long time. Tracey Orme showed great sympathy to the medium when taking the flat pictures. Diana Brinton, my editor, was encouraging and fun, and the staff at Anaya were endlessly patient and helpful when I was late with everything.

The Post Office have been a great hindrance in getting this book done at all.

The furniture was restored by Terence Walsh, Park Farm, Hook Norton, Banbury, Oxfordshire OX15 5LR (Tel. 0608 730 293), and the upholstery was undertaken by Mark Antony Bayliss, 167 Reading Road, Henley-on-Thames, Oxfordshire RG9 1DP. (Tel. 0491 574 893).